Bitter Water

and

Barren Lives

Restoring Broken Relationships Through Forgiveness

HEBREWS 12:15 *LOOKING DILIGENTLY LEST ANY MAN FAIL OF THE GRACE OF GOD; LEST ANY ROOT OF **BITTERNESS** SPRINGING UP TROUBLE YOU, AND THEREBY MANY BE DEFILED;*

by
Dr. W. Leon Sikes

Bitter Water and Barren Lives
©   Copyright 2010 by W. Leon Sikes

All Scripture quotations are taken from the King James translation of the Bible.

Additional copies of this book may be obtained by contacting;

Dr. W. Leon Sikes
101A Valley View Church Road
Harrison, Arkansas 72601
Phone 870-204-6876
e-mail - WLsikes@juno.com

ISBN # 978-0-615-34378-5
Library of Congress Control Number: 2010920183

Printed in the United States by Morris Publishing®
3212 East Highway 30
Kearney, NE 68847
1-800-650-7888

Dedicated to my loving and patient family.

To my loving wife Janice, who has traveled with me through all the trials of life for some 47 years while aptly performing all the duties of a wife and mother and honoring the unique position of "pastor's wife". To my great sons, Dennis, Doug, David and Dan, who lived in a "parsonage", and with a "preacher", most of their life. They had every opportunity to become angry and bitter but chose to be "content" in the environment in which God placed them. Last, but not least, to all the great "Christians" God has placed in my life and allowed me the opportunity to pastor, to learn from and minister to.

ACKNOWLEDGEMENTS

I really do not know where to begin in acknowledging all who have contributed to this book. First, and foremost I must acknowledge and thank my "Lord and Savior" Jesus Christ. Without Him there would be an unbelievable emptiness in my life and only despair for my future. He has made life an exciting adventure instead of a boring existence and made eternity a reality to anticipate ... not fear.

... I would like to think Dr. Charles Solomon who first introduced me to the areas of "Rejection" and "Bitterness" in the life of Christians. You will find his thoughts and materials scattered throughout this book.

... I must give a general thanks to all of the wonderful Church members, pastors, preachers and church staff who have been such a vital part of my life and ministry over the years. I claim nothing new or unique. Everything in this book came originally from the Word of God, through the ministry of the Holy Spirit and the final form is a compilation of thoughts, teaching and direction that I have received from the people God has put in my life.

Contents

Bitter Water and Barren Lives

Restoring Broken Relationships through *Forgiveness*

Introduction:

In *2Kings 2:19*, there is one of the most unusual and interesting stories in the Bible, and one I believe to be extremely relevant to today, to our society, and especially to our Churches. A delegation of officials from the historic city of Jericho had made a pilgrimage to find, and bring home, the prophet Elisha. Upon the delegation approaching their city, they paused on a hill outside of town, to help Elisha more fully understand their dilemma. As Elisha looked down from this observation point, he saw the city of Jericho as a lovely, fertile city, nestled on a small but luxuriant plain in the Jordan valley, but this was merely a facade. This plain was renowned for its abundance of plant life, including palm trees, fig trees, wheat fields, and beautiful wild flowers. All of these, nourished by the Jordan River, often called "the most interesting river on earth". It was here that the Israelite spies took refuge, as they were seeking to explore the land, and evaluate the people that they would soon conquer. The dilemma that the city faced was well hidden behind the facade of all this beauty, and productivity ... *the dilemma* ...... the abundant water was naught (***bitter)***, and the fertile land had become **barren**. The Hebrew word translated **barren** is ***shakol,*** which literally means to *miscarry*. This probably referred not only to the women, but also to the animals, and possibly the fruit and grain. Nothing would ripen! The bud would appear, followed by the blossom, and soon the fruit, but before it could ripen, it would be cast-off, *only* to die.

Introduction

I am afraid that we are confronted with this same scenario, in our lives, in our Churches, and in our society. To the entire world, we look fine. We are pleasant and peaceful, well dressed and well fed, but on the inside, we are filled with **bitterness** and **barrenness**.

We look very lovely and productive on the outside, but on the inside is a very different picture. Internally we are filled with **bitterness,** which is creating **barrenness,** in our life and ministry. Jesus said of the Pharisees that they were whitewashed on the outside, but like a lovely grave, they were filled with death on the inside. Though we do not like to admit it, this is sometimes a description of **us.**

In at least three places in God's word *(2Kings 2:19-22, Exodus 15:22-25 & James 3:9-12),* we find **bitterness** and **barrenness** linked together. It is apparent in each case that **bitterness** is the root cause of this **barrenness**. In *Hebrews 12:15* God warns us that a **bitter** root produces **bitter** fruit. Is your Christian life devoid of good fruit? Is it only producing **bitter** fruit? Do you often come close to victory, but end up in defeat? God indicates that **bitterness** is the cause of **barrenness,** and with that thought in mind, research carefully the material that I am going to share with you. Examine your own life, in the bright light of God's word, for any **bitterness** that you may have. From the beginning of creation, it has been God's plan that we be fruitful. **Bitterness** is often the wall that separates us from the fruitful life that God intended. Jesus said, *"I have come that you might have life, and that you might have it abundantly"*. Are you enjoying the abundant life, or are you struggling to survive, day by day. Struggling because of the acid called *BITTERNESS,* which is eating at your very being, and stealing your peace and productivity.

Bitterness is like me taking poison and waiting for the other person to die.

2

Chapter 1
The Causes of Bitterness

Bitterness can have many causes, but I believe that there are three root causes, based upon these Scripture references,
(2Kings 2:19-22, Exodus 15:22-25 & James 3:9-14)

CIRCUMSTANCES

In *2Kings 2:19-22* (*"And the men of the city said unto Elisha, Behold, I pray thee, the situation of this city is pleasant, as my lord seeth: but the water is **nought (bitter)**, and the ground **barren.**(20)And he said, Bring me a new cruse, and put salt therein. And they brought it to him.(21)And he went forth unto the spring of the waters, and cast the salt in there, and said, Thus saith the LORD, I have healed these waters; there shall not be from thence any more death or **barren** land.(22)So the waters were healed unto this day, according to the saying of Elisha which he spake."*) We discover that **bitterness** was brought about by <u>*CIRCUMSTANCES*</u> beyond the control of those who were its victims. Remember it is the *circumstances* that we cannot control, not the **bitterness** produced by these *circumstances*. We do not choose our *circumstances,* but we choose to be **bitter**! The water was plentiful, but not potable. In America we truly live in a land of plenty. On the outside our cities are often beautiful, and to the casual observer all looks well, while in the heart of that lovely city there is often crime, corruption, greed, and murder. We drive through a well-kept neighborhood, past freshly painted homes, with manicured lawns, multicolored flowerbeds, lush shrubs, towering trees, and we fail to observe that in those peaceful looking homes may reside, anger, adultery, incest, neglect, and abuse.

We see a handsome gentleman, or lovely lady walk by, and are often prone to envy. I dare say that in many incidences we would be repulsed rather than attracted if we could see what God sees ... the heart, the mind, the emotions, the soul, and the sin ... the real person inside that attractive house of clay.

The water is plentiful, but it is **bitter** because some alien component is affecting not only its taste, but is warping its mission. Water meant life, to these people, and is often called *"living water"*, in Scripture, because of its intrinsic attachment to life. In the Middle East, and at this time, they knew how vital *"good"* water was to life. In fact, even in America, fierce battles have been waged over water. Without water, there is no life, and without the *"living water"* of Jesus, there is no eternal life.

What are the circumstances that have turned your water bitter? Is it that God has not treated you fairly? Has He given someone else more than you? Has God made someone richer than you, someone who certainly did not work as hard as you did, and thereby does not deserve even as much as you do? Has God made someone more attractive than you are, more talented than you are? Does your neighbor live in a bigger home, drive a newer car, and have a better job? Maybe God just does not know how really deserving you are. What has turned your water **bitter**? Have other people treated you unfairly? Did your boss

4

give the raise, or promotion, to another person who is not nearly so talented, or hard working as you? Was everyone invited to the party, but you? Did everyone else receive recognition for his or her efforts, while you were ignored? There is a great deal of rejection in life, and this rejection can be broken down into two primary areas ... **covert** and **overt** ... listed below are some of the things that cause these two types of rejection to occur in our lives.

Overt rejection.

- Direct statements of rejection made by others.

- A refusal by others to show open affection.

- Actual verbal or physical abuse.

- Desertion by a parent, a child, a spouse, or a loved one.
- Divorce by your parents, or in your own marriage.
- Peer pressure due to some physical, mental, or emotional problems in your life.

Covert rejection.
- Unusually harsh or strict discipline.
- Unusually lax or erratic discipline.
- Over protection by parents, or spouse.
- Conditionally given love.
- Self-rejection due to misunderstanding God's purpose for your life.
- The death of a parent, child, spouse or loved one.

The causes of Bitterness

These areas of rejection in our life, when not properly dealt with, can create a great deal of **bitterness,** and can cause our life, and ministry to be **barren.** Since rejection is such a vital ingredient in the development of our bitterness, I would like to list some clues to discovering areas of rejection. This rejection may have produced **bitterness** in your life. Consider the following Scripture verses to help deal with this rejection, before it turns into **bitterness.**

⇒ A distrust of God and His plan for our lives -
   Psalms 139:14
⇒ Wishful comparison to others - *2Corinthians 12:12-18*

⇒ Self-contempt, and excessive self-criticism –
   Ephesians 5:29
⇒ Attitudes of superiority - *1Corinthians 4:6,7*

⇒ Excessive shyness, or feelings of inferiority -
   Philippians 4:13
⇒ Attempts at total perfection - *Philippians 3:12-14*

⇒ Unnatural attempts to hide unchangeable defects in the way
   God created us - *2Corinthians 12:9,10*
⇒ Extravagant dress, or mannerisms - *Matthew 6:27,28*

⇒ Difficulty in loving, and trusting others -
   Matthew 19:19
⇒ Unbiblical priorities, and goals in life - *Matthew 6:33*

Signs of victory are everywhere, but the results in your life are still negative. The trees had blossomed, the fruit appeared, only to fall to the ground unripe, and then lay there to rot. The cattle had conceived, only to miscarry, and abort their young before there was any possibility of sustaining life. The women had conceived, but in the midst of celebrating the joy of this new life coming into the world, spontaneous abortion occurred, taking the life of the child, and the joy of the parents in one fell swoop.

Yes, *CIRCUMSTANCES*, over which we have little or no control, can, turn our water **bitter** and poisonous, but there is other sources of **bitterness**, as well.

LACK OF FAITH

Another major cause of **bitterness** is a *LACK OF FAITH*, according to *Exodus 15:22-25("So Moses brought Israel from the Red sea, and they went out into the wilderness of Shur; and they went three days in the wilderness, and found no water.(23)And when they came to Marah (bitter), they could not drink of the waters of Marah, for they were **bitter**: therefore the name of it was called Marah.(24)And the people **murmured** (refused to go any farther) against Moses, saying, What shall we drink? (25) And he cried unto the LORD; and the LORD showed him a tree, which when he had cast into the waters, the waters were made sweet: there he made for them a statute and an ordinance, and there he proved them"),*. While we have little control over circumstances, we can exercise much control over our faith. How does a *LACK OF FAITH* produce bitterness? Well let's look at the Israelites, and their lapse of faith. This condition was brought about primarily because they forgot the past, and I think this is exactly what happens to us. God had just performed one of the greatest miracles in the Bible. He had parted the Red Sea. Stood it on edge like two giant walls reaching into Heaven, while the Jews (between 3 and 5 million), walked across on dry land *(Exodus 14:21,22)*. In a few days, however, their joy had turned from *MIRACLE* to *MURMURING*

MURMURING (Exodus 15:24). God had just delivered them from death. God knew exactly where they were, where they were going, and what they needed to get there, but they were not content to live by faith. In fact, they wanted to stop following God and return to Egypt. It has been my experience that trials bring either confidence in God, or **bitterness** toward God. Trials tend to make us **bitter** or **better**. How have the trials in your life influenced you?

What has God done for you in the past? If you are a Christian, He has saved and preserved your soul for eternity, and promised you abundant life here and now. If He NEVER does anything else, that should be enough to cause rejoicing in our life rather than **bitterness**. Paul said, *"Finally, brethren, whatsoever things are true, whatsoever things are honest, whatsoever things are just, whatsoever things are pure, whatsoever things are lovely, whatsoever things are of good report; if there be any virtue, and if there be any praise **think on these things**." (Philippians 4:8)*. Remember what God has done, before you start worrying and fretting over what He needs to do. This is a *LACK OF FAITH*.

UNGODLY LIFE STYLE

There is a third major source of **Bitterness** and **barrenness,** which the Bible identifies as an *UNGODLY LIFE STYLE*. In James 3:9-18, *("Therewith bless we God, even the Father; and therewith curse we men, which are made after the similitude of God. (10) Out of the same mouth proceedeth blessing and **cursing**. My brethren, these things ought not so to be. (11) Doth a fountain send forth at the same place sweet water and **bitter**? (12) Can the fig tree, my brethren, bear olive berries? either a vine, figs? so can no fountain both yield salt water,* *and fresh. (13) Who is a wise man and endued with knowledge among you? let him show out of a good conversation his works with meekness of wisdom. (14) But if ye have **bitter** envying and strife in your hearts, glory not, and lie not against the truth. (15) This wisdom descendeth not from above, but is earthly, sensual, devilish. (16) For where envying and strife is, there is confusion and every **evil work**. (17) But the wisdom that is from above is first pure, then peaceable, gentle, and easy to be entreated, full of mercy and good **fruits**, without partiality, and without hypocrisy. (18) And the **fruit** of righteousness is sown in peace of them that make peace. ")* our Lord's brother reminds us of some areas in our life where we must surrender control to God, or risk stepping into the snare of **bitterness**. I believe that we all have two distinct alternatives in life. We can let God **_run_** our life, or we can **_ru̇in_** our life.

The choice is ours. I have already made mine.
"As for me, and my house we will serve the Lord".

THE TONGUE

Let's examine some areas of control that God deems necessary to a healthy <u>CHRISTIAN LIFE STYLE,</u> and ministry. First, God wants control of our *tongue*. In verse eight of chapter three in James' letter he says, *"the tongue can no man tame; it is an unruly evil, full of deadly **poison**."* Since we cannot control our *tongue*, it would seem obvious that we need to let God have control. This is the case, by the way, in every area of our life. A *tongue* out of control is like a fire out of control. It will wreak havoc and destruction until control comes. The *tongue* releases what the mind stores, and we often have things stored in our mind that should never be released upon the world, and more importantly, upon our loved ones.

BEHAVIOR

Another thing in our life that God wants to control is our *behavior (James 3:13)*. *Behavior* is a product of our will, and until we submit our will, to Gods will, our *behavior* will be a constant cause of **bitterness**. In *Hebrews 12:15*, God says that **bitterness** troubles us and defiles many. We cannot separate our *behavior* from our **bitterness**. Just as what is in the mind leaks out through the mouth, by virtue of the tongue, the **bitterness** in our life leaks out through our *behavior*. I do not believe in self-control for the Christian. I believe in Christ control. Until we let Christ control our *behavior* it will be a source of trouble, confusion, and **bitterness**. God always loves me, and His love does not change nor diminish because of my *behavior*, but He does not always love my *behavior*. He often allows me to suffer the terrible consequences of my *behavior*, while He continues to love *me*.

ATTITUDE

There is yet a third thing that produces an UNGODLY LIFESTYLE, and that is failure to control our *attitude (James 3:14)*. Everything rises and falls on *attitude*. Paul in *Philippians 2:5* says, *"Let this mind (attitude) be in you, which was also in Christ Jesus"*. Everything begins with *attitude*. One of the first things a pilot learns about flying is the necessity to achieve the right *attitude*, (not altitude) for his airplane. The reason for this is simple. The wrong attitude will cause the plane to crash, and the same is true in our Christian life. The wrong *attitude* will cause us to *crash!*

Attitude also determines our understanding, and response to *guilt*, and how we deal with the *guilt* in our lives. This <u>guilt</u> can be a very strong, contributing factor, to **bitterness**. There are actually two kinds of *guilt* that we have to deal with. There is *real guilt*, which is the result of actually violating the law of God, and there is *imaginary guilt*, which is the result of doing something that you have been erroneously taught is contrary to the law of God. It can be something you have decided is wrong, but God has nothing to say about it. Strange as it may seem, the solution for both is the same. Thinking that something is a sin, and then doing it, actually makes it sin, since this is open rebellion toward God. God says, "If we confess our sins, He is faithful and just to forgive us our sins, and to cleanse us from all unrighteousness." *1John 1:9*

As you can quickly determine, these are all problems that occur in the area of our *SOUL*. They relate to our mind (*what we know*), our will (*what we do*), and our emotions (*what we feel*). Even though these problems often affect us physically and spiritually they are in reality mental and emotional battles, fought in the arena of our soul.

Please look through the following lists that relate to areas of rejection and check any that apply to you. Rejection is as common as dirt and involves all aspects of life and living. The fact of rejection is not the problem. The problem is how we respond to the rejection that occurs in our life. The purpose for checking those that apply is so that they become more real to you and help you to understand how many of these acts of rejection have actually occurred in your life. These areas of rejection that relate to your life may be possible sources of anger and bitterness that will need to be dealt with in your life.

BIRTH
IT IS REJECTION WHEN . . . . .

☐ Your mom had a terribly difficult delivery, and she constantly reminds you how she went to death's door to give you life.

☐ Your parents wanted a boy, and you came instead.

☐ Your parents wanted a girl, and you disappointed them.

☐ You were told that you were conceived accidentally.

☐ You were a late-in-life baby, and were expected to bring new joy into your parents' marriage.

☐ You were a late-in-life baby, and your parents were in their 60's when you were a teenager.

☐ Your dad was not with your mom, when she delivered you.

☐ Your mom miscarried before, or after your birth.

☐ Your dad didn't help mom with you, when you were a new baby.

☐ You were born with a birth defect.

☐ You were born out of wedlock.

☐ You are a twin, and never got to celebrate your own birthday.

☐ You are a twin, and always had to wear matching clothes.

☐ You were born prematurely, and separated at birth from mom.

FAMILY
IT IS REJECTION WHEN . . . . .

☐ As a child, I had to wear hand-me-downs all the time.

☐ As a child, I was called names, such as dumb, stupid, brat, idiot.

☐ As a child, I could never dress as nice as other children.

☐ As a child, I always had to wear the nicest clothes, and keep perfectly clean.

☐ My mom and dad were always fighting.

☐ My mom and dad never talked.

☐ My mom and dad started a fight in front of the kids, settled the argument in private, and did not let the kids know that they had reconciled.

☐ My parents criticized each other in front of the children.

☐ My parents depend on me to help them solve their adult problems.

☐ I was not allowed to be a child.

☐ I was never left with a baby sitter or left alone when I was older.

☐ I was given the message, "I'll never leave you", and then the parents divorced, or died.

☐ I was told to be seen, and not hear.

☐ My dad never/seldom took a vacation with the family.

☐ My dad and mom did not attend school functions.

☐ I was given a nickname that made fun of some physical problem (ie; "Bucky" due to buckteeth, "Chubs" due to excessive weight, "Skinny" due to sub-normal weight).

☐ I was not allowed to get my driver's license until I was eighteen and most of my friends were driving at age 16.

☐ As the oldest child, I had the responsibility for the younger children.

☐ As the oldest child, I had to do all the work, while the younger ones played.

☐ I was reared in extreme poverty, or wealth.

☐ As a middle child, I was neglected.

☐ My youngest sibling was babied, pampered, and overprotected.

☐ My dad and/or mom were alcoholics.

☐ My dad and/or mom used drugs.

☐ My dad and/or mom were workaholics.

☐ My dad and/or mom put the kids first, and neglected each other.

☐ My mom/dad handled all the problems at school. One of my parents did all the discipline.

☐ My parents yelled at us children.

☐ My parents never spent time with me individually.

BITTER WATER AND BARREN LIVES

- [ ] My dad never laughed.

- [ ] My mom never smiled.

- [ ] I was expected to carry on with the family business, when I had other goals, I wanted to pursue.

- [ ] I was expected to go to college, and be something that I did not want to be.

- [ ] I was not allowed to make mistakes.

- [ ] I was told to do my schoolwork, so I could be a better person, than my parents.

- [ ] As a teenager I was never allowed to choose my own dress style.

- [ ] I had a learning disorder.

- [ ] I had a bed-wetting problem.

- [ ] I had a severe sickness that I did not understand.

- [ ] I was too tall for my age.

- [ ] I was too short for my age.

- [ ] I had severe acne as a teen.

- [ ] I do not remember getting hugged.

- [ ] I had to work long hours at a job, and could not spend time with my friends.

- [ ] I was given everything I wanted.

- [ ] I was ten years old and Mom was still combing my hair/tying my shoes.

- [ ] Mom overprotected us and would not let us learn to make our own decisions.

MARRIAGE
IT IS REJECTION WHEN ......

☐ I cannot have a close, same sex, friend outside the marriage.

☐ My spouse has too many friends, or activities outside the marriage.

☐ My spouse is quiet, and withdrawn.

☐ My spouse is demanding, and hostile.

☐ My spouse is a workaholic, and never spends time with me.

☐ My spouse is sexually, or emotionally unfaithful.

☐ My spouse criticizes me in public.

☐ My spouse withholds affection, and praise.

☐ The words "*I love you*", or "*I appreciate you*", or "*thank you*", or "*I am sorry*", are seldom/never used.

☐ The in-laws live with us, or we live with the in-laws.

☐ Sex is used as a weapon, or bribe by my spouse.

☐ Silence is used as a weapon, by my spouse.

☐ I must always agree with my spouse.

☐ My husband/wife never calls while he/she is away on business.

☐ I am never allowed to "get away from it all", by myself.

☐ My mate is extremely possessive, or jealous of me.

☐ We have no quiet time together, except for sex.

☐ The Lord is not the head of our family.

☐ My spouse praises other people, but seldom me.

SEX
IT IS REJECTION WHEN.......

☐ Sex was never discussed in an open and healthy manner with my parents.

☐ I started my menstrual cycle, and thought I was bleeding to death.

☐ I began puberty, and was teased because of getting pubic hair.

☐ I was given a perception that sex was dirty.

☐ I developed prematurely, and became the brunt of jokes from my peers.

☐ I came out of puberty underdeveloped.

☐ As a teen I would give sex to gain acceptance.

☐ I was molested, or raped as a child, or young person.

☐ I was always told that sex is wrong, but suddenly on my wedding night, it was supposed to be perfectly fine.

☐ I was told as a child that masturbation was an evil sin.

☐ As a teen, I never once masturbated.

☐ Nudity was made a big issue, even as a young child.

☐ Nudity is excessive, and modesty is not taught.

☐ In my marriage, sex is withheld, or used as a bribe.

☐ In my marriage, sex is never discussed in an open, and healthy manner.

☐ My husband/wife is much more interested in sex than I am.

☐ I am not fulfilled, in my sexual relationship, with my spouse.

FINANCES
IT IS REJECTION WHEN ... ...

☐ There was never enough money as a child, and you always heard about it.

☐ Dad always griped about how much money he spent on the family.

BITTER WATER AND BARREN LIVES

- [ ] You work, and your money is yours, and your spouse's money is theirs.
- [ ] The bills are never paid on time.
- [ ] One spouse handles all the finances, and the other is kept in the dark.
- [ ] You criticize your husband's ability to make money.
- [ ] You criticize your wife for not making any money.
- [ ] As a child you never received an allowance.
- [ ] You do not give your children an allowance.
- [ ] You had to earn every penny your parents gave you.
- [ ] Your children have to earn every dime you give them.
- [ ] Your parents gave you everything, and never expected you to be responsible for anything.
- [ ] You never make your children earn any of their spending money.
- [ ] Your husband expects you to turn your paycheck over to him, and you get nothing.
- [ ] Your parents help one child financially, and not the others.
- [ ] There's never enough money for the husband and wife to get away for the weekend, or go out to dinner together.
- [ ] Your husband complains about the money he spends on you.

☐ Your wife complains she never has anything to spend.

☐ As a wife you work to provide for the family.

☐ Your husband can never seem to find the right job, or hold on to the job he has.

DIVORCE
IT IS REJECTION WHEN .....

☐ One of your parents blames you for their divorce.

☐ One parent, for taking the other parent's side, criticizes you.

☐ As a child, you had to decide which parent to spend the holidays with.

☐ As a spouse you wonder, "Did I do enough? Did I do everything possible?"

☐ You feel that you have deserted the children because you do not have full custody.

☐ Since you now have custody of the children, you feel like you must now play the roles of both mother and father.

☐ Your spouse, who has custody, will not care for the children properly.

☐ As the absent spouse, you are ignoring the children's needs.

☐ As the absent spouse, you desire more time with the children, as they are maturing.

☐ Your previous spouse begins to undermine the authority, discipline, or genuine love and concern of the new step-parent, toward their children.

☐ As a wife that has seldom/never worked outside the home, and has helped her husband get his education, and build his career, you suddenly become a non-entity in the relationship

RE-MARRIAGE
IT IS REJECTION WHEN ....

☐ Your new spouse withholds total commitment, for fear of getting hurt.

☐ The children are made a more important priority, than the new spouse.

☐ The step-parent tries to discipline the step-children.

☐ The spouse in a second marriage, claims ownership of his/her material goods, and feels they are not to be shared with the new spouse, or stepchildren.

☐ There is rivalry among the children, and you take your own child's side.

☐ There are activities for your step-child, but none for you, with your spouse.

☐ Your new spouse complains about the money that is spent on your own children's needs.

☐ Your new spouse feels unwanted by your old friends.

☐ You feel unwanted by your new spouse's old friends.

☐ Your new spouse feels unwanted by your relatives.

☐ You feel unwanted by your new in-laws.

☐ Your new spouse feels that they cannot measure up to providing materially, or emotionally, as the previous spouse.

☐ The previous spouse demands time, and attention, which creates hostility with your new spouse.

☐ As a child of divorce, you had to re-adjust to your new step-parent, after spending time with the absent natural parent.

☐ The natural parent defends the child's wrong behavior, to the new stepparent.

☐ Your new spouse has a disturbing habit, which was hidden until after marriage.

☐ The actions of your new spouse, reminds you of behavior in your former spouse, that you could not tolerate.

☐ Your new spouse accuses you of being just like their former spouse.

CHURCH
IT IS REJECTION WHEN .....

☐ You get saved, and are asked, "How do you feel now?" (you may not feel anything)

☐ You feel guilty without knowing the Biblical basis (there is real guilt [sin] and imaginary guilt).

☐ Your spirituality is measured solely on your outward actions.

☐ You are made to feel "backslidden", if you don't show up for every service.

☐ You are part of a legalistic church.

☐ You feel guilty if you don't participate in all church activities.

☐ You are criticized because you don't believe God wants you to be a teacher, or officer, or deacon in the Church.

☐ You are labeled as "not full of the Holy Ghost" if you don't speak in "*tongues*".

☐ Your Christian gift is not understood.

☐ You feel that you must disagree with the leadership of the Church, and they will not listen to you.

☐ Your involvement in Church is to gain acceptance.

☐ Church involvement becomes an outside support system, for a bad marriage.

☐ Parents never spend a weekend away, with their children, because they are always in church.

☐ You have to dress, and act, like everyone else in the Church.

Chapter 2

The Identifying Signs of Bitterness

If this whole book was dedicated to identifying signs of **bitterness** it would fall short. Obviously this short chapter will not go into great detail, however, we will attempt to look at, and summarize, the foundational signs, that identify **bitterness**.

AVOIDANCE

I truly believe that the first and most obvious sign, that we are harboring **bitterness** or resentment toward someone, or something is our *avoidance* of that person or thing in our life. We turn our back, we look the other way, we avoid eye contact, we move across the room, or across the street, all in an attempt to avoid any intimate contact. We work at avoiding social, recreational, work and even Church contacts wherever possible. We cringe when the phone rings, and bristle when we see someone or something that resembles, or reminds us of the person or thing that we are **bitter** toward. Throughout the Bible we are instructed to confront rather than *avoid* problems. Modern psychology says that there are at least three types of emotional responses to situations in our life. We can be *passive* (just let everything slide), we can be *aggressive* (just attack everything) ...... or we can be *assertive* ..... and confront each issue with honesty, and integrity as God instructs us in - Ephesians 4:15 "*...telling the truth in love.*"

It is obvious what path the Christian must take. Not the path of least resistance, or the path of most resistance, but the path that leads to reconciliation, and peace.

ANGER

I believe that there is another very obvious "sign" in our life that reveals **bitterness**. This particular problem can be best described as *continual anger.* Are you always angry? Do the smallest problems seem to set you off? Do you continually fight, and bicker with those closest to you? If these things seem to define your life, then you need to begin a serious search for **bitterness** in your life. **Bitterness** can sometimes be elusive, and hard to find, however, it is most often very easily discovered, and clearly identified. Most often it is found in our attitude toward the very people, or things we avoid. As you begin your **bitterness** search, look for people who intimidate you, and people who have wounded your spirit through hurtful acts. Remember, *anger*, and irritability are only symptoms of a much deeper problem, and this problem could well be *bitterness of the soul.*

SELF DEFENSE

Another symptom of **bitterness** can be detected in our attempt to recruit allies to our *defense.* We begin to build our own empire, and recruit our own army. The Bible, especially the Psalms, teaches us that God is our ally, our strong defense, our shelter, our high tower, and etc. If God be for us, who can be against us?

Christian you do not need to recruit allies for your *defense*. You need to turn your *defense* over to your personal attorney, Jesus Christ. He will defend us as no other attorney and He will also be quick to point out, where we are in the wrong, so that our agenda is always in line with His.

COMMUNICATION

When we refuse to instigate, or participate in *communication*, I believe that this is another obvious sign of **bitterness** in our life. We withdraw from a particular person, or place, or thing, because we know, inherently, that we will be drawn into an argument, or conflict, due to the **bitterness** in our own soul. Even when **bitterness** is not recognized on the conscious level, we are always aware, in our soul, that it exists, and that it will be a constant source of irritation to our life, and to our Spiritual maturity. Remember this, *WE CANNOT, **NOT** COMMUNICATE. Communication* is on so many levels that it is impossible to totally avoid it. A look, a gesture, a shrug all says something. In fact silence can often speak the loudest of all.

Communication problems are only the fruit, of a root problem, called **bitterness**. When **bitterness** is removed from our life, most of our *communication* problem will go with it.

REVENGE

The last sign of **bitterness**, which we will deal with, is our desire for *revenge,* which usually shows up in the form of personal attacks. It is vital that we remember what the Lord said, - Romans 12:19 - ... *"Vengeance is mine, I will repay"*...

When you think about *revenge*, it is only logical to conclude that we can never really *GET EVEN*. We are always behind, or ahead in our attempt at *revenge*. We have never done enough to get even, until we finally do too much, and then we feel guilty about that. Just let God, in his ultimate wisdom and justice, even out the score. Personalities, or fear, or intimidation, or anger, or power, or money, or position, or any of the other things that tend to shade our decisions and influence our actions, never influence God's decisions. God always decides and determines based on His integrity not our desire.

Chapter 3
The Wrong Response to Bitterness

W e are creatures of **response**. The problem being, that too often, our response is incorrect, overbearing, or too passive for the situation. In this chapter let's look at the wrong responses to bitterness in our life.

JUSTIFY OUR BEHAVIOR

One of the first things we do when confronted with the **bitterness** and resentment in our lives is to *justify* it to ourselves, and to those around us. As we discuss this reaction, please remember that, *"your problem, is not your problem, your problem, is how you respond to your problem"*. Everyone has, basically, the same problems in life. How we deal with these problems determines our level of **bitterness.** Jesus, from the cruel cross of Calvary, chose to forgive those who had created His problem, even though He had every right to be bitter, angry, and resentful. He knew that becoming bitter would destroy everything He had worked to accomplish the last thirty-three years of His life. Jesus could have *justified* anything because He was totally without fault, yet He chose to forgive, and refused to be bitter.

SIT, SOAK AND SOUR IN SELF-PITY

When we are not busy trying to justify our **bitterness** and resentment we like to spend time in *self-pity*. We throw a "pity party" and celebrate our miserable condition. One thing to keep in mind during a "pity party", is to never invite anyone else, especially someone who cares about you, they can ruin the whole party. *Self-pity* is a very singular activity, and demands solitude, and situational control. When you get around other people, particularly other Christians, they have a tendency to try and encourage you. This can be a devastating blow to an otherwise successful "pity party". *Self-pity* is not the answer to **bitterness,** and in fact is the wrong answer to any problem in the life of a Christian.

IGNORE THE PROBLEM

If justifying our **bitterness,** or having a good old fashioned "pity party" is not the solution to the problem, we often decide to just *ignore it,* or pretend it really doesn't exist. This solution is about as successful as pretending that it is not hot in Phoenix in the summer, it is not wet in Houston in the winter, and that people never disagree on anything. **Bitterness** is real, and it is harmful, and God commands us not to be **bitter.** If **bitterness** doesn't exist, then God's Word becomes foolish for instructing us about the dangers of this soul poison. Face the fact that you are probably harboring some **bitterness,** and instead of denying it, face up to it, and discover what God has to say about getting it out of your life.

LIVE WITH THE CONDITION

Often times we listen to the advice of the world, and the psychology of Satan, and decide we will learn to simply *live with* the condition. Remember that *living with* bitterness is like *living with* some terminal disease, for which there is a cure. God has provided a cure for our **bitterness,** and it seems so foolish to try and *"live with"* this disease that is destroying our life and ministry. Often the cure for a disease causes as much pain as the malady itself, but seldom is the cure more painful than the disease. I have an injured shoulder and every few years I have to go in and let the Doctor give me a cortisone shot. These really hurt but nothing compared to the pain in my shoulder, and does it feel really good when the pain stops. At any rate, if the disease is terminal, then the cure is mandated, no matter how painful it may be. Covering over **bitterness,** is like putting dirt on the weeds in your garden. Before long you have a big mound of dirt, and a strong, healthy weed popping through that mound of earth. If you want to get rid of the weeds, pull them up by the roots. If you want to get rid of bitterness, pull it out by the roots. *Hebrews 12:15* *"Looking diligently lest any man fail of the grace of God; lest any **root of bitterness** springing up trouble you, and thereby many be defiled;"*

ATTACK

Another normal tendency with bitterness is to *attack* the person, or thing that created this **bitterness** in our life. Again this is the world's philosophy, and is contrary to the Word of God (*Romans 12:19*). **Bitterness** is our problem not theirs. It is not what others have done to us, but how we have responded to their offenses. If you have allowed them to make you **bitter,** then you are in sin, and must seek God's forgiveness and their forgiveness for your attitude. I know that this is a strange and perhaps foreign concept, even to Christians. As we continue you will understand exactly where I am coming from, and where we need to go, with God's doctrine of forgiveness.

INVOLVE OTHERS

One of the worst responses we can have to **bitterness** is to involve *others* in our conflict. Often they are not a part of the problem, or the solution, and this causes them to take up an offense (*Psalms 15:3*) against one, or both of the parties. Then they become **bitter** themselves. Never involve *others*, who are not a vital part of the problem, or the solution. When *others*, who are not directly involved, are brought into the conflict, they have an unusual dilemma. They have no real way to resolve the conflict that develops, in their own life, because they were not initially involved in the dispute. Getting *others* involved only expands the problem, and makes the entire situation worse. We never do *others* a favor by involving them in problems that do not concern them, even if it is only to pray for us. We all have a tendency to take sides, and this has a way of magnifying the problem, and expanding the **bitterness**.

The last thing I want to look at is the difficulty we have in trying to deal with **bitterness,** when we don't have a proper understanding of God's methods for dealing with this poison of the soul. The Bible is very clear, but the world, the flesh, and the Devil have been quite effective in distorting God's plan of reconciliation. The reasons for this are obvious. When Christians are reconciled to God, and to one another, they become very productive for the Kingdom of God. Satan hates productive Christians, and churches, and will do anything to stop the reconciliation that brings this to pass. If America is going to see revival it must experience reconciliation in homes, families, churches, and etc. Make sure you understand, and practice what God's word says about the reconciliation required to remove **bitterness** and **barrenness** from your life.

Chapter 4
The Consequences of Bitterness

There are so many consequences associated with **bitterness** and **barrenness**, that it will be most productive, and understandable if we divide them into the three parts of man. .... Physical, Mental, and Spiritual. Just as God is a Trinity, He made man a Tri-unity in His likeness and image.

Physical

Physically, **bitterness** can have some devastating consequences. The *stress* that **bitterness** creates in our physical being can produce a chemical imbalance that adversely affects the adrenal, thyroid, and pituitary glands as well as many organs, including the heart, lungs, stomach, and liver. When these glands produce too many or too few hormones they affect the body, in a negative way. Like an automobile racing from traffic light to traffic light, flooring the accelerator, and then stomping on the brake pedal. This type of driving soon wears out our tires, brakes, and adversely affects the engine. Driving our body in the same manner, soon wears out, or damages many of its components. **Bitterness** can show up in our facial expressions (*Nehemiah 2:2,3 & Proverbs 15:13*) and according to God's word even affect our blood supply (*Proverbs 14:30 & 17:22*) by attacking the bone marrow, which produces our blood.

Mental & Emotional

Mentally and emotionally, **bitterness** can create stress, depression, phobias, delusions and sundry other maladies, due to our "emotional focus" on one person or thing. This "emotional focus" is usually on an individual or incident that caused us great distress. In essence this means that the focus of our life is on an individual, or incident, that we really dislike. Consequently that person, or thing, becomes the controlling factor in our life. It consumes our time, energy, and passion. We take this controller to work, to play, to bed, and to church. Who do you want controlling your life? Do you want someone, or something that hurt you to rule and run your life, or do you want Jesus Christ to be the Lord of your life.. There is an excellent book, written several years ago, by S. I. McMillen; M.D., titled, *"None of These Diseases"* that deals with many of the maladies that stress and **bitterness** brings into our lives. Now let's look at the Spiritual aspect of our **bitterness**.

Spiritual

Spiritually, **bitterness** is a sin. In *Hebrews 12:15* God commands us not to be bitter, and shares some of the spiritual consequences of **bitterness**. God says, "**bitterness**...... troubles you, and .... many are defiled" by its affect on you. In *Ephesians 4:31* He says, "Let all **bitterness**..... be put away from you, with all malice." and in *Colossians 3:19* He says, "Husbands, love your wives, and be not bitter against them." **Bitterness** can best be defined as an inward resentment, or unresolved anger. Jesus said very clearly in *Matthew 22:37-40* that we are to love Him and love our neighbor like ourselves.

I would like to take this a step further and say that if we do not love ourselves unconditionally, and our neighbor unconditionally, we cannot love God unconditionally, and this puts us in violation of the **great commandment**. John says that if we do not love our brother whom we can see, how can we say that we love God whom we have never seen (*1John 4:20*). Consequently we build a barrier of un-forgiveness between God and us. In *Matthew 5:22-26* God says that reconciliation is essential;

❶ For worship   ❷ For fellowship   ❸ For blessings

It has been said that the difference between **bitterness** and **joy,** is our capacity for forgiveness. I do not know who, or what, has hurt you, and caused bitterness in your life, but I do know, you need to get rid of it. Sometimes a laugh, a smile, or a joke, is simply a facade for covering a flood of bitter tears in the soul. Maybe you were abused …. sexually, physically, emotionally, mentally, or etc …… as a child. Perhaps a dear friend, or colleague, or even a stranger has hurt you deeply. Has your life been shattered by the death, divorce, separation, or severe rejection by someone you love? Did you get passed over for a promotion ….. has your character been assassinated by someone you trusted ….. have you been betrayed by a spouse. Please understand that *hurts* and *rejection* comes in many forms, and shapes, and occur continually in every life. They are real, frustrating, and painful. Often those around us do not understand, or seem to care. Remember what I said earlier in the book, **"your problem is not your problem, your problem is how you respond to your problem".** There are at least three common responses to most problems;

- We can *internalize* them and end up **bitter**.
- We can *retaliate,* and end up **bitter**.
- We can *forgive,* and end up with **joy** in our life.

> Good advice for dealing with hurts, "When you get hurt, don't curse it, don't rehearse it, don't nurse it, just reverse it, by giving it to Jesus."

We have already discussed the first two responses in detail, lets now look at some Bible characters who chose this third response, (we can forgive, and end up with joy in our life) to the hurt and rejection in their life. Each one had ample reasons to become bitter, but all determined to choose the *"high road"* and forgive.

JOSEPH was attacked, and sold into slavery by his own brothers. He was falsely accused by Pharaoh's wife, and thrown into prison. He was forgotten by a man who promised to remember him, and help him ..... but ..... Joseph chose not to be bitter, and ended up second in command of all of Egypt where he became the savior of his father, and the very brothers who initially betrayed him. (*Genesis 47:11,12*)

JOB was attacked by the devil, and lost everything he had; his children, his possessions, his health, his dignity, his influence, his friends, and even his wife turned on him .... but ..... Job chose not to be bitter, and everything he lost was restored when he prayed for the very ones that had hurt him. (*Job 42:10-13*)

JESUS was attacked by the devil, and His own people; He was despised, rejected, abandoned, tried in a kangaroo court, mocked, beaten, spit on, crucified, and buried ..... but ...... Jesus chose not to be bitter. From the cross of Calvary, while in pain and agony, He said, "Father forgive them; for they know not what they do." *(Luke 23:34)*

STEPHEN was attacked by a vicious mob of his own people; he was beaten, cursed, and stoned ..... but ...... Stephen chose not to be bitter. Kneeling before this rabid mob of murderers, he asked God not to charge them with the terrible crime they were committing against him. *(Acts 7:60)*

Someone or something has hurt you, and you have succumbed to **bitterness**. This is natural and normal, but God asks us to be supernatural and abnormal, by following the example of our Savior, Jesus Christ. Hurts can make you *better* or *bitter*, the choice is yours. We would certainly hate to have a toxic waste dump in the back yard of our home, yet it seems like we are willing to allow the poison and acid of **bitterness**, to reside in the front yard of our mind and life. Choose this day to deal with your **bitterness**, and begin to experience the *joy* that God promised you. Overcome the **bitterness** in your life by doing what God tells you to do, in His word.

Before we begin this exciting and exhausting journey through *forgiveness* there are some things we can do to prepare for this emotional roller coaster. We need first to commit to an absolute trust in the word of God and total cooperation with the Holy Spirit as he carefully guides us through the entire process. Jesus promised us His *peace* in ways that we can barely imagine.

(John 14:27) ***Peace*** *I leave with you, my **peace** I give unto you: not as the world giveth, give I unto you. Let not your heart be troubled, neither let it be afraid.*

(Philippians 4:7) *"And the **peace** of God, which passeth all understanding, shall keep your hearts and minds through Christ Jesus."*

(1 Thessalonians 5:23) *"And the very God of **peace** sanctify you wholly; and I pray God your whole spirit and soul and body be preserved blameless unto the coming of our Lord Jesus Christ."*

Peace is one of the Fruits of the Spirit and as with all of the gifts of God we must be willing to reach out by faith and appropriate this gift into our life. I truly believe that we could sit under an apple tree, with our mouth open, and starve to death waiting for an apple to somehow fall into it. God's peace is the same way.... we must reach out by faith, pick it up and make it a part of our life. God gives it to us, it is ours and we must now accept it by faith.

God also needs to make some adjustments in our Mind and in our Emotions. Our mind simply constitutes what we know and our emotions are how we feel about what we know. It is not at all unusual to have a huge disparity between what we believe and what we feel about a particular subject or event that has occurred in our life.

For instance;

I know that I am a good husband, but I don't feel like a good husband.

I know that I am a good wife, but I don't feel like a good wife.

I know that I am a good dad, but I don't feel like a good dad.

I know that I am a good mom, but I don't feel like a good mom.

I know that I can do that, but I don't feel like I can do it.

I know that he/she loves me, but I don't feel like he/she loves me.

I know that God has forgiven me, but I don't feel like I am forgiven.

The Bible teaches us that God can do some amazing surgical adjustment to these two areas of our soul, by using the knife of His word. In Hebrews 4:12 God says, *"For the word of God is quick, and powerful, and sharper than any twoedged sword, piercing even to the dividing asunder of soul and spirit, and of the joints and marrow (body), and is a discerner of the thoughts (mind) and intents (emotions) of the heart."*

HOW WE FEEL

Let me begin by explaining what I mean when suggesting that we need some biblical adjustment to our Emotional (how we *feel*) structure. The most damaging emotion that we deal with is our resentment or bitterness toward people or circumstances in our life. We will deal with this bitterness by first understanding what **bitterness** really is. It is simply *unresolved anger* that has festered and turned into *inward resentment*. It begins with an *incident*, over which we get *angry*, our anger is *not resolved* and that anger then becomes **bitterness**. Remember that bitterness literally defiles or poisons our emotions.

Lets look at what some various authors in the New Testament have to say about bitterness:

Hebrews 12:14, 15 - *"Follow peace with all men, and holiness, without which no man shall see the Lord: (15) Looking diligently lest any man fail of the grace of God; lest any root of **bitterness** springing up trouble you, and thereby many be defiled;."*

Acts 8:23 - *"For I perceive that thou art in the gall of **bitterness**, and in the bond of iniquity."*

Ephesians 4:31, 32 - *"Let all **bitterness**, and wrath, and anger, and clamour, and evil speaking, be put away from you, with all malice: And be ye kind one to another, tenderhearted, forgiving one another, even as God for Christ's sake hath forgiven you."*

WHAT WE KNOW

The second area of adjustment is our intellect or our mind (what we know). The primary need in the area of intellect is our **attitude**. I truly believe that everything rises and falls on **attitude** and from Scripture it is obvious that God is vitally concerned about our **attitude**.
In fact God states that we are to have the very **attitude** of Christ:

Philippians 2:5 - *Let this **mind** (attitude) be in you, which was also in Christ Jesus:*

Ephesians 4:23 - *and be renewed in the spirit of your **mind** (attitude);*

Romans 12:1, 2 - *I beseech you therefore, brethren, by the mercies of God, that ye present your bodies a living sacrifice, holy, acceptable unto God, which is your reasonable service. (2) And be not conformed [quit being conformed] to this world: but be ye transformed by the renewing of your **mind**, that ye may prove what is that good, and acceptable, and perfect, will of God.*

I believe that our objective in adjusting both our mind (what we know) and our emotions (how we feel) must be centered on understanding and allowing God to change our "emotional response patterns". Emotional response patterns were discussed in detail in Chapter 3. A simple definition of our "emotional response patterns" is that they are the way in which we respond emotionally to what ever occurs in our live. These responses become *"emotional response habits"*.

These can then become *"emotional response sins"* as we continue to nurture them instead of resisting. Obviously not every response pattern is a sinful one and the good responses need to be nurtured. I am only concerned about the bad response patterns that adversely affect our lives and relationships. Let's take a detailed look at how Paul defines these "sinful response patterns" in his letter to the Church at Rome. It is clear from the writings of Paul that this was a serious problem in his personal life. Why are these response patterns so important to our life? Because they control a large percentage of our overall behavior and in one way or another they affect every one of us. Let's listen to Paul as he struggles with these responses in his life:

Romans 7:15-25 - *[15]"For that which I do I allow not: for what I would, that do I not; but what I hate, that do I. [16]If then I do that which I would not, I consent unto the law that it is good. [17]Now then it is no more I that do it, but sin [sinful response patterns] that dwelleth in me. [18]For I know that in me (that is, in my flesh,) dwelleth no good thing: for to will is present with me; but how to perform that which is good I find not. [19]For the good that I would I do not: but the evil which I would not, that I do. [20]Now if I do that I would not, it is no more I that do it, but sin [sinful response patterns] that dwelleth in me. [21]I find then a law [law of sin], that, when I would do good, evil is present with me. [22]For I delight in the law of God after the inward man: [23]But I see another law [law of sin] in my members, warring against the law of my mind, and bringing me into captivity to the law of sin which is in my members. [24]O wretched man that I am! who shall deliver me from the body of this death?*

[25]I thank God through Jesus Christ our Lord [the answer]. So then with the mind I myself serve the law of God; but with the flesh the law of sin [sinful responses]."

(The [*bracketed*] words are my addition and not to be taken as Scripture)

If you would like a really interesting comparison of the victory over these *"sinful response patterns"* in the life of the Apostle Paul, read Philippians Chapter 4. There is probably a five-year span between the writing of these two letters and they reveal how Paul allowed **Jesus to be the answer**. After finishing the exercises in the next chapter you need to turn your life and behavior over to the Holy Spirit of God and allow Him to begin producing His fruit in your life and stop trying to do it on your own.

Galatians 5:22 – *"But the fruit of the Spirit is love, joy, peace, longsuffering, gentleness, goodness, faith, (23) Meekness, temperance: against such there is no **law**."*

Chapter 5
Overcoming Bitterness

W e overcome **bitterness** through **forgiveness.** Forgiveness is a judicial act of the will. We did not deserve, nor could we ever deserve forgiveness from God, yet He chooses to forgive us, and cleanse us from all unrighteousness, when we choose to receive His Son as our Savior. This is simply a judicial act of His will, whereby He chooses to justify, and declare us innocent upon the merit of His Son. We **must** approach forgiveness in the same manner that God does. In *Matthew 6:14, 15* Jesus goes so far as to say that our forgiveness from the Father is dependent upon our forgiveness of those who offend us. Back in Chapter 5 and verse 44 He describes what this forgiveness entails;

⇒ *Love your enemies.*

⇒ *Bless them that curse you.*

⇒ *Do good to them that hate you.*

⇒ *Pray for them that despitefully use you, and persecute you*

Based on Jesus' teaching in Matthew and throughout the New Testament let's explore some of the excuses that cause us such great difficulty in forgiving others.

I REALLY HAVE NO ONE I NEED TO FORGIVE!

Has anyone ever hurt you? Have you ever been rejected, lied to, treated unfairly, cheated, stolen from, belittled, abandoned, humiliated, slandered, abused (physically, mentally, sexually)? Have you gone through the tragedy of divorce, dealt with an unfaithful spouse, been hurt by a rebellious child, neglected by an alcoholic parent, or uncaring, grown children. If any of these things are true please check the appropriate statements on the following pages so that they become more real and thus easier to deal with;

Have you ever;

☐ been lied to

☐ had a promise broken

☐ been neglected by grown children/siblings/parents

☐ had a violent crime committed against you

☐ been treated unfairly by an employer

☐ had parents get divorced

☐ been slandered/falsely accused

☐ been divorced

☐ had a spouse commit adultery (physically or emotionally)

☐ been stolen from

☐ been abused (physically, emotionally, or sexually)

☐ been cheated in a business/financial deal

☐ been publicly humiliated

☐ been rejected by your parents

☐ been abandoned by parents or spouse

☐ had alcoholic parents or spouse

☐ been belittled (especially in public)

☐ had a rebellious/wayward son or daughter

As you look at all the ways in which you have been offended, are any of these statements true about you.

☹ I have a secret (or maybe open) desire to get even, for the offense against me.

☹ I really don't care if the offender has to suffer, for what they did to me.

☹ I have a pressing need to tell others, about how I have been hurt.

☹ When I see someone, or something that reminds me of the offense, I become angry.

☹ I am not able, to truly thank God, for the person, or thing that deeply hurt me.

If you answered yes to any of these statements, then you have not truly, and fully released the offender from the debt, you believe they owe you, and thus you have not really forgiven them. Remember that forgiveness is a judicial act of the will, whereby I fully release the offender from their debt, and from this point forward I will never bring up this offense to God, to others, or to the offender themselves. Based on *1John 1:8,* what is my response to the following statement?

I admit that there is un-forgiveness in my heart.
❑Yes ❑No

Some excuses we use for refusing to forgive.

THEY DO NOT DESERVE FORGIVENESS!

Does anyone deserve to be forgiven by God, considering how we have treated Him and His Son Jesus? Based upon *Romans 5:8,* God chose to love us, forgive us, and save us while we were still in sin, and enemies of Him and His Son. In Ephesians 4:32, He says, *".... be ye kind one to another, tenderhearted, forgiving one another, even as God for Christ's sake hath forgiven you."* We are to forgive because God commands it, and because we have been forgiven! **That is reason enough.**
What can we do to deserve God's forgiveness? *Romans 5:8 & Ephesians 2:4-9*

Which of these are the proper reasons for forgiving those who sin against us?

☐ The offender is sincerely sorry for what they have done.

☐ God forgave me, and thus I must forgive as I have been forgiven.

☐ God commands me to forgive.

☐ The offender promised never to do this again.

☐ The offense was an "understandable mistake" on their part.

I HAVE BEEN HURT TOO DEEPLY TO FORGIVE!

When we begin to discuss hurts, we must always compare our hurts to the suffering of Christ, and to the apostles and disciples of old. Have we been beaten, stoned, shipwrecked, or crucified? For most of us, our suffering has been minimal compared to Christ, and the martyrs of history. Even today, there are untold thousands on foreign soil, who are suffering unbelievable atrocities. In the Word of God you might look at *Isaiah 53:3-7,* and *Psalms 22:6,7,16,* along with *Matthew 26 & 27; Mark 14 & 15; Luke 22 & 23*, and *John 18 & 19* in the New Testament to get a clear picture of the suffering endured by our loving Savior. Even after all of this, He forgave those who had so viciously attacked, condemned, and crucified Him.

It is important to examine the reaction of our Savior to hurts and suffering, but it is equally important to examine His commandments to us, concerning how we handle the hurts in our life.

BITTER WATER AND BARREN LIVES

How are we to react to those people, or things that hurt us? *Luke 17:3,4* says that we are to love them, and do good to them. In *Romans 12:17-21* the Apostle Paul says not to seek revenge, live peaceable, give your enemy food and drink, and overcome evil with good. Paul also says, in *Colossians 3:13*, that we are to be patient, and forgiving in the same way as Christ.

What are some ways in which Jesus suffered at the hand of mankind?

◊   *Isaiah 53:3-7*

_____

_____

◊   *Psalms 22:6-16*

_____

_____

What has God done about those who treated His Son in such a horrible way?

◊   *Ephesians 2:4,5*

_____

◊   *Isaiah 43:25 & Hebrews 10:17*

_____

_____

◊   *Micah 7:18,19*

_____

What did Jesus say was the proper response to those who offend us?

◊   *Luke 6:27*

_____

◊   *Romans 12:17-21*

_____

◊   *colossians 3:13*

_____

◊   *Luke 17:3,4*

_____

What should be the standard, by which we measure our forgiveness of others?

◊   *Colossians 3:13*_____

By that standard, what sin is "too great" for **us** to forgive?

_____

How does God enable us to do such a "difficult" thing?

◊   *Philippians 4:13*

_____

I WILL FORGIVE, BUT I CAN NEVER FORGET!

When God forgives us He does some special things with our sin.

▪ *Micah 7:19* says He

▪ *Isaiah 38:17* says He

▪ *Psalms 103:12* says He

▪ *Hebrews 10:17* says He

Remember this is what God does, not what He asks us to do.

Understand that forgiveness is a judicial, and deliberate act of the will, whereby we release the offender from their debt to us. This is exactly what God did, when He chose to forgive us, and give to us eternal life. Some people are confused by God's statement in *Jeremiah 31:34* and *Hebrews 10:17* where He says, "I will remember their sin no more." God, through His omnipotence, chooses to never again remember the sins that He has forgiven. **He** can do this! We cannot! Besides it is profitable that we remember. It is these memories that keep us from repeating sins, and tragedies of the past.

51

God also uses our memory to help us test our forgiveness of others. How do you feel when the memories of some "hurtful" incident come seeping into your consciousness? Does your stomach begin to churn? Does your heart beat faster? Is revenge still a viable option? Do you have trouble seeing any good in this person, or situation? Do you really want everyone else to know just exactly what they did? If these reactions are common, then forgiveness is not accomplished. On the other hand if you truly desire to see the person who hurt you, restored spiritually. If you can truly rejoice when God blesses them. If you are truly thankful that God allowed the hurt to occur so that you might grow spiritually through the offense. Then you can know that forgiveness is fully accomplished, and you can get on with your life and ministry for Christ.

The attitude of our heart is often an excellent barometer to determine if we have truly forgiven another. When you remember the offense, which of these reactions do you have?

Normal Reaction

☐ an emotional churning.

☐ a desire for revenge.

☐ difficulty in asking God to bless them.

☐ difficulty in seeing their good qualities.

☐ a desire for others to know the wrong they did.

Biblical Reaction

☐ a desire for God to bless them.

☐ a desire to see them restored.

☐ a sense of rest and peace.

☐ a gratefulness to God for this person.

☐ a humbling due to the immensity of the sin that God forgave in your life.

I HAVE TRULY FORGIVEN, BUT I STILL HURT!

You still hurt because of what we just discussed. You have not, and cannot **forget** the offense you suffered. Like any open wound to the soul, you must allow the ointment of God's healing love to cauterize and cure this injury. Forgiveness is the essential starting place in our relationship with God, and with others, but it is *just the beginning*. There is much restoration, and rebuilding ahead if we are to turn something painful into something productive. If we are to move from **bitter** to **better** we have much prayer, scripture reading, and hard work ahead. Now is the prime opportunity to return "good for evil", to practice loving your enemy until they become your friend, and learn to turn the other cheek until your neck becomes sore.

God tells us that there are some things we need to do beyond forgiveness.
In *Luke 6:27-31* He tells us to;

In *Romans 12:17-21* He tells us to;

_____

_____

_____

_____

After forgiveness, God asks us to make a positive investment in their life. This is the key to experiencing emotional healing, and wholeness in our own life. If possible, God desires that we seek to rebuild the relationship between ourselves, and the offender. If this is impossible, or not appropriate (in the case of a former spouse, or etc) we can still invest in their lives through praying for them. Please list some practical ways in which you can invest in the life of someone who has wronged you.

_____

_____

_____

_____

I REFUSE TO FORGIVE!

I truly believe that life, and Christianity is filled with choices. We choose to receive Christ as Savior. We choose to let Him be Lord of our life. We choose to be obedient to His Word, and we choose to forgive our enemies, and those who hurt us in this life. As I understand the Word of God, forgiveness is a matter of choice, but it is also a matter of necessity. Unless we forgive others, God will not forgive us. (*Matthew 6:14, 15*) Jesus, in answer to Peter's question in *Matthew 18:21-35* gives us a concise thesis on the subject of forgiveness.

He says first that there is really no limit to the number of times we are expected to forgive. Secondly, the size of the offense is not important, but the act of forgiveness is crucial. Jesus then talks about turning an individual, who refused to forgive, over to the tormentors. I am not certain what is meant by the term tormentors, but I do understand enough to know I want no part of this discipline by God. It seems that my life has enough natural tormentors without me going out of my way to appropriate more. I believe I'll choose the path of forgiveness. How about you? If we choose not to forgive what does God say that we can expect from Him.

☹ *Matthew 6:14, 15*

☹ *2Corinthians 2:10, 11*

☹ *Matthew 18:32-35*

55

As I said earlier, I do not know exactly what God means when He says tormentors in *Matthew 18:34,* but I do know that the Greek term used literally means, *"the one who inflicts torture"*. What are some of the physical, emotional, mental, and Spiritual "tormentors" that we might expect to experience in our lives if we are unwilling to forgive?

FORGIVENESS CAN BE DIVIDED INTO SEVERAL VITAL STEPS OF ACTION:

❶　In sincere prayer, share with God, that you choose to forgive everyone who has ever offended, hurt, or deeply disappointed you, and mention each to God, by name, rehearsing the offense to God, as you ask God to forgive them.

Confess any sin in your life that you are aware of, and ask God for His forgiveness.

> ⇒ Immorality
> ⇒ Anger
> ⇒ Bitterness
> ⇒ Dishonesty
> ⇒ Etc.

❸ Make a list of every person that you have sinned against and begin asking them personally for their forgiveness:

One of the first sins to deal with is the sin of **bitterness**. Because this sin is usually most prevalent, and resolving it, will usually take care of many other sin issues in your life, I recommend that it be at the top of the list. Make a complete list of people you have become **bitter** toward, listing especially those whom you avoid, or who intimidate you. Remember, this sin is affecting your life, and ministry, and causing you to be barren in the service of God. Keep in mind; it is not the offense that matters, but your reaction to that offense.

No matter what the offense, if it has made you **bitter**, then that is **"sin"** in your life and you must seek forgiveness for this sin (your **bitterness**). Under no circumstances should you ever say to anyone..."*I forgive you for what you have done*"... unless they specifically ask for that forgiveness. When you offer the forgiveness before they are ready to seek it, you have placed yourself in a superior position, spiritually. When you contact someone personally, to seek forgiveness for your **bitterness**, I would suggest that you do it by telephone, if at all possible. The reason for this is simple. The telephone allows you control of the conversation. Do not be drawn into a discussion about how they offended you. This is counterproductive, and may even make the situation worse. Keep the conversation simple, and to the point. Have a quiet and meek spirit. Begin by asking them to forgive you for your **bitterness** (resentment) toward them. If they hesitate, or attempt to circumvent the request, ask again. Do this, at least three times, and if they still refuse, or try to alter the course of the conversation, just say, in a meek and loving way, *"I have turned your response over to God, and I appreciate your willingness to talk with me; thank you and good by"*. Hang up the phone gently, and do not answer it for a while, in case they call back. Remember they are not totally aware of what you are trying to accomplish. Remember also that they may be *bitter* toward you.

Start with your own family; Husband/wife, children, parents, and other relatives. Move to friends, acquaintances, and coworkers. Some of those who have caused **bitterness** in your life may be deceased. In this case write a letter to them, voicing all your anger, frustration, hurt, and etc., then ask them for forgiveness for your **bitterness** toward them. After writing the letter, give it to someone you trust completely, and someone who loves you, ask them to read it, and then destroy the letter entirely.

The reason for this is so that someone who cares for you can hear your hurt, and your request for forgiveness. If at all possible, this other person should be your spouse. There is one other area of **bitterness** that needs to be addressed, and that is **bitterness** toward God. I think that this is a lot more common than Christians care to admit. Realize, if you are **bitter** toward God, He already knows it. In the case of **bitterness** toward God, you need to tell Him exactly how you feel, and why you became **bitter** (He already knows), and then humbly seek His forgiveness. Ask for His strength and wisdom to never fall into this deadly trap again.

After you have dealt with these areas of bitterness, everything else will probably be easy. You must, however, continue to pursue forgiveness from all the individuals that you have offended.

Chapter 5

Developing Christ-esteem

After you have dealt with the bitterness in your life, you need to learn how to **receive** rejection without **reacting** to it in a negative, and unscriptural manner. This will stop bitterness in your life, before it begins. In chapter No. 1 we dealt with the causes of rejection in our lives, both OVERT & COVERT, and the evidence that rejection is a prevalent part of our lives. The fact that you have been rejected is not important. What is important is how you handle that rejection. Has rejection made you **better** or **bitter**? Believe it or not the choice is yours. No one can make you **bitter**. **Bitterness** comes as a result of adverse reaction to rejection. Rejection is a fact of life! You cannot drive down the street without rejection. Even something as simple as a traffic signal is a form of rejection. In my counseling sessions, I tell people that they have at least three alternatives when stopped by a red light. They can carefully look in every direction, and then "run" the light, taking a chance on getting hurt, getting killed, getting a ticket, or getting away with it. The second alternative is to go home, get a shotgun, and come back to shoot, and destroy the light for stopping you. This can also have dire consequences. The third, and I believe best alternative, is to simply, wait patiently for the light to turn green, and then cross the intersection cautiously. I lived, for a while, in Southern California where even a green light, doesn't mean it is safe to cross the street. We need to always remind ourselves, that it is of little comfort, to have the words *"He Had the Right of Way"* etched on our tombstone.

Rejection can be devastating, or it can be a source of opportunity for Spiritual growth in our lives. Rejection is like a pot of rice, boiling over and spilling out onto the stove, because the burner cannot be turned off. Picture the steam, and rice pouring out onto the stove as the *symptoms* of rejection in our life. The unquenchable heat is the *source* of rejection, which cannot be stopped or turned off. This leaves us with the contents of the pot, which are the *problems* caused by rejection. It is what's in the pot that is making the mess. The solution is simple! Remove the pot from the burner and the problem ceases to get any worse, however, there is still a mess to clean up. When you remove the pot (problems) from the burner (source), the boiling over (symptoms) stops instantly. With this scenario in mind let's move to the real thing. If you have been adversely reacting to rejection in your life, your life is boiling over, and making a real mess.

Take the pot off the burner. Stop the symptoms by receiving the rejection, without adversely reacting to it.

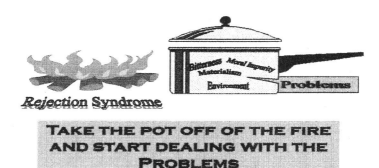

Rejection Syndrome

TAKE THE POT OFF OF THE FIRE AND START DEALING WITH THE PROBLEMS

Then begin to clean up the mess. Below is a list of some positive steps toward cleaning up the rejection mess in our life.

❶ Discover any areas of ungratefulness, in your own life, toward God.
  A. List everything about you that you would like to change.
  B. List the advantages for each of these areas of ungratefulness.

❷ Truly thank God for the way He made you, and learn to glory in unchangeable areas of your life that have been labeled *defects* by you or others.   *2Corinthians 12:7-10*
  A. Make these areas the marks of God's ownership. (*Galatians 6:17*)
  B. Make these areas your motivation to develop inward, and spiritual qualities.

❸ Allow God to finish the good work He has begun in you.   (*Philippians 1:6, 3:12-14*)

❹ Dedicate yourself to serving Christ, through serving others. Begin to allow God to reproduce His life, and character in you, and those around you.

There are also some definite things to do, regarding those people, or things that have rejected you. First and foremost be very cautious about blaming yourself for the rejection. This sets you up for self-rejection, and when you reject the self that God made, you are rejecting God, and establishing *yourself*, as Lord of your life (that is idol worship). As you deal with the rejection, fostered upon you by others, learn to trust God's love and protection. Realize that He is working to change both of you. Never be ashamed to seek outside help, but make sure the offender remains anonymous. Deal with the offense and the offense only. Nothing is gained through accusations, and you run a definite risk of hurting the person, who is seeking to help you (by causing them to take up an offense). When personalities, rather than incidents, are brought into the mix, there is a definite possibility of someone else taking up an offense, and succumbing to bitterness. Finally when dealing with those who reject you, ask God to help you love them, unconditionally, just as He loves you. Read carefully through *1Corinthians 13:4-7* and you will get a clear definition of what God means when He talks about love. Understanding love will help you to better deal with rejection in your life.

It has been my experience, that in our modern society, and perhaps all through history, there have been three things that seem to *color* our response to rejection.

MORAL IMPURITY

First and foremost is **_moral impurity_** in our own life, or in God's words, *"there is sin in our life"*. Remember that sins come in all sizes, and we tend to overlook the ones in our life, that we consider to be very small. In God's sight, all sin is the same size, and He overlooks **none**. (James 2:*10* - *"For whosoever shall keep the whole law, and yet offend in one point, he is guilty of all"*). For the sake of our study, however, lets look at what we like to consider big and little sins. A promise made, and not kept, is often, in our mind, a little sin, (lie) but when this promise was the one you made at the marriage altar, it can suddenly become a big sin (adultery). Sin in our life has a real tendency to determine the way we handle rejection. Sin causes us to be on the defensive, and thus each rejection is blown out of proportion. Before you attempt to deal with rejection, you need to deal with the *sin* in your life.

ENVIRONMENT

The **second** area that has a big impact on our response to rejection is our **_environmental development,_** or simply our background. Things like our physical appearance; height, weight, coloring, complexion, and body proportions can set us up as an easy prey for rejection. Our God given abilities and talents are also a set-up for rejection, especially when we forget that all abilities and talents come from God, and He is only interested in how we use them. We live in a day and age when most people are oversensitive about the value others place on these things. A big part of our environment is totally uncontrollable. We do not choose our parents, our race, our nationality, or the place of our birth, yet we often let these things adversely affect our life, and determine how we deal with rejection in our life.

Please understand, God knew the environment in which you would be born before you were even conceived. He determined what you would look like, and decided in eternity past which talents, personality and abilities you would have (Psalms 139:14 – *"I will praise thee; for I am fearfully and wonderfully made:"*).

SELF ESTEEM

We hear much about self-esteem or self-image, and how it affects us, and our lives, but for the Christians there should be **no** self-image, only Christ's image or what I call Christ-esteem (Philippians 2:5 - *Let this mind be in you, which was also in Christ Jesus:"*). Godliness/humility is not based on a low or negative self-image; it is based on **no** self-image... only a Christ-image. A negative self-image is merely a negative image of Christ's work in our creation, whereas a positive Christ-image is a positive perception of Christ's marvelous work. He created us, and gave to us the gifts, talents, and abilities that we have. To help us develop a positive Christ-image in our life we need to have confidence in God's will for our life (Romans 8:28 – *"And we know that all things work together for good to them that love God, to them who are the called according to his purpose"*). We need to look forward to the future God has planned for us, with a positive anticipation, (Philippians 4:13 – *"I can do all things through Christ which strengtheneth me"*). and we need to learn how to unconditional accept ourselves the way God does. (Ephesians 1:6 – *"To the praise of the glory of his grace, wherein he hath made us accepted in the beloved"*). When we allow Satan to produce a negative self-image in our life we succumb to feelings of inferiority, insecurity, and inadequacy because we "compare" ourselves to those around us, instead of looking to Christ we fail to love ourselves unconditionally as Christ loves us, and consequently we have difficulty loving others, and worst of all we find it difficult to love God ….. **unconditionally**.

FIVE CONSEQUENCES OF A NEGATIVE SELF- IMAGE:

❶ AN INABILITY TO FULLY TRUST GOD:

We teach that God is maker, and creator of everything, including us. We believe that He is a God of infinite love and wisdom. Yet we are disappointed in how He has made us, and what He is doing in our lives. On some level of consciousness we have a tendency to believe that if what we are is the best God can do, then we are in real trouble. The problem with this kind of thinking is that we ignore what God is really doing in our life. We fail to comprehend that we are a work in *progress*, not a finished *product*. Often times these feelings are as much a product of our lack of faith in who we really are, as it is a lack of faith in what God can/will do in our life. God says, "we are a chosen generation, a royal priesthood, a holy nation, a very special people who were called from darkness into light". *(1Peter 2:9)* Isn't it strange that we are willing to trust Christ with our eternal soul, but unwilling to trust Him with the daily circumstances of our life.

❷ AN INHERENT RESISTANCE AGAINST ALL AUTHORITY:

A rejection of who we are creates a natural rejection of God, and His authority, in our lives. This then tends to spill out into every other area of authority, in our life. Since God is the ultimate authority, and He has disappointed us, how much more will lesser authorities, bring hurt into our life. Consciously, or unconsciously we begin to develop the attitude that God, and everyone else owes us something. We see this clearly demonstrated in the world around us. Everyone is screaming for his or her rights. For access to what they deserve, and for recognition for who they are. This may be fine for the world, but in Christianity, there is no room for such self-centered thinking. With God we have no rights, only privileges granted by a Savior who loves us so much that He says, (John 14:13 - *"And whatsoever ye shall ask in my name, that will I do, that the Father may be glorified in the Son")*. I would much prefer to ask God for privileges, than go before Him demanding my rights. This feeling of being *"short changed"* by God can often become what I call *"floating bitterness"*. This floating bitterness moves from rebellion, and anger toward God, to rebellion, and anger toward all authority that we perceive to be in God's chain of command. This would include parents, spouses, employers, teachers, pastors, and etc.

❸ A DETERRENT TO DEEP AND ABIDING RELATIONSHIPS:

This rejection of God, and all authority figures, creates an atmosphere of distrust that permeates our relationship with everyone else in our life. We become overly sensitive to how others respond to our appearance, our talents, and our background. This concentration on the unchangeable facets of our life, keeps us from concentrating on the spiritual, emotional, and physical needs of others, which is the basis for real, and lasting relationships. Often times, these negative feelings about ourselves, leads us to constant *self-criticism*. We do this with the hope that others will contradict us, and boast about us, or we develop a facade of superiority and sophistication that makes it difficult for others to be comfortable around us. When we do not love and accept ourselves, it is extremely difficult for others to love and accept us.

❹ A DISTRACTION FROM OUR REAL ACHIEVEMENTS:

Real achievement, in the life of a Christian, is allowing God to develop inward qualities that make us more like Him (2Corinthians 3:18 – *"But we all, with open face beholding as in a glass the glory of the Lord, are changed into the same image from glory to glory, even as by the Spirit of the Lord"*).

Our problem, so often, is that we concentrate more on pleasing men than pleasing God. We certainly need to love others, and forgive others, and live peaceably with others, but nowhere does God say that we must please others. If others accept us, just as God made us, that is wonderful, but if they don't, it is their problem, not ours. Our desire to gain the approval of men can often be a detriment to gaining the approval of God. It also thwarts the purpose that God uniquely designed us to accomplish in our life and ministry. 1Samuel 16:7 says, *"... for man looketh on the outward appearance, but the LORD looketh on the heart."* God is looking on the inside while man looks at the outside. Ultimately what we are on the inside will reveal itself in our outward attitude, actions and appearance, but our concern must always be on the heart. Where the heart leads, the hand will follow.

❺ A VERY STRONG EMPHASIS ON MATERIALISM:

Materialism is almost as hard to define as humility. There can often be a very fine line between needs and wants. The line is so hard to define, in some instances, that we need to seek God's ruling in our life. On the other hand, materialism can easily be detected in the way we live and act. It can show up in the home we own, the car we drive, the clothes we wear, and the things we impulsively buy. Money is not evil, only the love of money. Possessions are not evil, only coveting the possessions of others. Saving is not evil, (in fact the Bible instructs us to be good stewards in 1Corinthians 4:2 – *"Moreover it is required in stewards, that a man be found faithful."*) but hoarding is (Luke 12:20 –*"But God said unto him, Thou **fool**, this night thy soul shall be required of thee: then whose shall those things be, which thou hast provided?"*). You need to realize also, that rejection can reveal its ugly nature in self-debasing. This is brought about by dressing down, trying to appear unattractive, and jumping on the band wagon of every ridiculous, and sometimes obscene fad and fashion that comes along. We are not what we wear, what we own, or even how we look. We are what God sees on the inside, and that is what needs to be the central focus of life.

HOW DO WE DEVELOP CHRIST-ESTEEM?

A positive **Christ-image** requires a new and different relationship with God. This relationship must be personal and intimate. We must first know Him as our **LORD** and **SAVIOR**, and then we must unconditionally surrender to His workmanship in our life (Ephesians 2:10 – *"For we are his workmanship, created in Christ Jesus unto good works, which God hath before ordained that we should walk in them"*). We must also, and always, realize that He is far from finished with us. (Philippians 1:6 - *Being confident of this very thing, that he which hath begun a good work in you will perform it until the day of Jesus Christ:"*). This new relationship must have absolute confidence in God's will for our life (Romans 8:28) – *"And we know that all things work together for good to them that love God, to them who are the called according to his purpose"*). God is revealing Himself through our lives, much like an artist, reveals himself through his art. We must, therefore, allow God to express His will through the *"canvas"* of our lives, and refrain from grabbing the brush out of God's hand, and making amateurish strokes on the *"portrait"* of our life. This relationship must be in total cooperation with His plan for our life - (2Corinthians 1:4 – *"Who comforteth us in all our tribulation, that we may be able to comfort them which are in any trouble, by the comfort wherewith we ourselves are comforted of God"*). We must have the **attitude** of Christ - *(Philippians 2:5),* as we allow ourselves to be conformed to the **image** of Christ through the work and ministry of the Holy Spirit (Romans 8:29 – *"For whom he did foreknow, he also did predestinate to be **conformed** to the image of his Son, that he might be the firstborn among many brethren"* & Romans 12:2- *"be not conformed to this world: but be ye **transformed** by the renewing of your mind, that ye may prove what is that good, and acceptable, and perfect, will of God"*). This will transform us by the renewing of our mind. It will transform our attitude, and our actions. We will look at everything differently. Our response to people and situations will be more Christ like, and we will behave in a manner that draws men to Christ, instead of turning them away from Him.

I believe that there is a simple formula for developing Christ-esteem in our life.

First we need to learn how to be thankful to God, for everything in our life. (Ephesians 5:20 - *"And are built upon the foundation of the apostles and prophets, Jesus Christ himself being the chief corner stone;"*).

It is vital that you verbalize, to God, **gratefulness** for your problems, for any unchangeable defects or deficiencies in your life, and for any area of your life that you previously resented, including persons, places, or things.

__Secondly__ we need to determine who is responsible for the problems, circumstances, and conditions in our life. There are only three alternatives ... **God, you or somebody else** ... If it is God, you need to thank Him and ask Him what He would have you do, to resolve the problem. If it is you, then you need to change the attitude, behavior, or circumstances (if possible) that created the problem. Ask God to help you refrain from getting back into the same situation. If it is somebody else, then ask God how you can use the circumstance to minister to him or her.

__Third__, we should attempt to discover what God is trying to teach us, and when we discern this, begin applying the lesson to our life on a daily basis.

(A suggestion to help you develop Christ-esteem in your life.)

Put the following prayer on a 3x5 card;

---

1. Thank you Lord for my problems.
2. Help me accept and love myself, **unconditionally**, as you do.
3. I promise that I will cooperate with you as you remodel and rebuild my life.

Pray this prayer, every evening for 21 days
(If you miss a day, start over!)

BITTER WATER AND BARREN LIVES

This prayer will help you learn to **receive** but not **respond** to rejection in your life. Remember, **"Your problem is not your problem, your problem is how you _respond_ to your problem".** As you pray this prayer and practice the principles of forgiveness that we have discussed the following Scripture will help you to make this a way of life. (2Corinthians 3:18) - *"But we all, with open face beholding as in a glass the glory of the Lord, are changed into the same image from glory to glory, even as by the Spirit of the Lord."*
Below is my very casual interpretation of this verse.

(The more I look at Jesus, the more I look like Jesus, and the more I look at the world, the more I look like the world.)

Chapter 7

Discovering God's <u>Purpose</u> In our <u>Problems</u>

*Remember, your **problem** is not your **problem**; your **problem** is how you respond to your **problem**.*

<u>SELF</u>

We have three sources for all of our problems. The first source is <u>**OUR SELF**</u>. God made us a tri-unity (body, soul, and spirit) and each of these parts can be a source of problems in our life, and ministry. Without Christ, we have a *fatal* flaw, in that our spirit is dead and our soul is condemned to Hell. Even with Christ as Savior, we can have great conflicts in our soul. Our soul is made up of our Mind (what we know), our Emotions (what we feel), and our Will (what we do). What we know (our mind), can have conflict with what we feel (our emotions), and this situation adversely affects what we do (our will). Thus we behave in ways that destroy our testimony for Christ, our quality of life, and prevents our ministry from being productive.

ENVIRONMENT

The *second* source of our problems involves our **ENVIRONMENT**. There are many facets of our environment that can cause great frustration. Our family, our career, our friends, and the society, in which we live, can all be a source of great frustration, and emotional problems in our life and ministry. Always trust that "all things work together for good", *(Romans 8:28)* and that there is a positive purpose for the environment in which God has placed you. It may be that you have a ministry in that location, or with those particular people, where you can be more effective than anyone else. Are you willing to lose the blessing of God on your ministry, for a more comfortable environment in your life?

OTHER PEOPLE

The *third* source of our problems is simply other **PEOPLE**. People in general can be a real source of irritation. For the most part, they do not think like we do, act like we do, nor agree with us on every issue of life. Their behavior is often unacceptable, their personalities are sometimes abrasive, and they can often be very inconsiderate towards us. If we allow these God given differences to affect or destroy, our ministry for Christ, then we have become the pawns of Satan, and he, subsequently, becomes the god of our life. God says that we are to love others, and that love is defined in (John 3:16 – *"For God so loved the world, that he gave his only begotten Son, that whosoever believeth in him should not perish, but have everlasting life."* - where God says "that love is the willingness to give to meet the needs of others, without asking anything in return". Remember that love is an action, not an emotion. We can literally love people whom we do not like. I have found, however, that if I love someone and pray for him or her, it becomes much easier to like them. Some people are very lovable and easy to love, while others are very unlovable and difficult to love, but like Jesus, we must love even the unlovely.

There is a way to eliminate all of our problems. Just eliminate the sources. As ridiculous as this sounds, people sometimes attempt this very method. People commit suicide, move and change locations constantly, or even try to eliminate the people in their lives.

Problems fall into two primary classifications.

Problems that are solvable. - *Philippians 4:13*

1. **We can change our HABITS.**

2. **We can transform our ATTITUDE.**

3. **We can gain control over our CONDITIONS.**

4. **We can improve our ABILITIES.**

5. **We can alter our CAREERS.**

Problems that we cannot change. -
2Corinthians 12:7-10

God uses these problems to reveal the sufficiency of His grace, to develop our character, and to produce inward qualities, which make us more like Christ. Remember, problems in our life are simply opportunities for us to see God work. When we fail to respond in a positive way to our problems, we thwart the very purpose of God, in allowing us to have the problem. When we respond incorrectly, God must then allow more and sometimes more difficult, problems to occur in our life, so He can continue to mold us into the image of Christ. - *Romans 8:29* - When we respond correctly, God is free to remove the problem, solve the problem, or give us grace to live with the problem. - Proverbs 16:7 – *"When a man's ways please the LORD, he maketh even his enemies to be at peace with him."*

Let's examine some of the improper reactions to the problems in our life.

We **Blame** the problem on someone else. - Romans 14:12 – *"So then every one of us shall give account of himself to God."* It has been said, "We are never truly a failure until we blame someone else, for our situation in life." Even if someone else is to blame, the problem is now ours to deal with. Concentrate on your **attitude**, not their **actions**.

- We **Defend** ourselves. - Romans 12:19 – *"Dearly beloved, avenge not yourselves, but rather give place unto wrath: for it is written, Vengeance is mine; I will repay, saith the Lord."* If we are right, we need no defense, other than God. If we are wrong, we have no defense, we only need God's mercy.

- We **Hold** everything inside. – Ephesians 4:26 – *"Be ye angry, and sin not: let not the sun go down upon your wrath:"* **Bitterness** or resentment is simply, unresolved anger. Christ says that we are to resolve conflicts quickly. - Matthew 5:25 – *"Agree with thine adversary quickly, whiles thou art in the way with him; lest at any time the adversary deliver thee to the judge, and the judge deliver thee to the officer, and thou be cast into prison."*

- We immediately **Tell** our problems to everyone. - Proverbs 29:20 – *"Seest thou a man that is hasty in his words? there is more hope of a fool than of him."* This only makes the problem worse, and more widespread. It can also cause others to take up an offense. Make sure you do not involve anyone, who is not a part of the problem, or a part of the solution.

- We **Withdraw** from the problem, or from God, or from those who can give wise counsel. Proverbs 11:14 – *"Where no counsel is, the people fall: but in the multitude of counsellors there is safety."* Problems must be dealt with in a proper and timely manner.

Here is a simple formula for handling problems in your life.

- ◊ Don't curse them. - Anger only makes them bigger.
- ◊ Don't rehearse them.- This only causes them to grow and spread.
- ◊ Don't nurse them. - This creates or increases self-pity.
- ◊ Disperse them. - Give them to God; He knows just how to handle them.

◊ Reverse them. - Use them for Growth - 2Corinthians 1:4 – *"Who comforteth us in all our tribulation, that we may be able to comfort them which are in any trouble, by the comfort wherewith we ourselves are comforted of God."* & Genesis 50:20 – *"But as for you, ye thought evil against me; but God meant it unto good, to bring to pass, as it is this day, to save much people alive."*

Let's examine some Biblical responses to the problems in our life.

① *First* we must sincerely **thank** God for our problems. Ephesians 5:20 – *"Giving thanks always for all things unto God and the Father in the name of our Lord Jesus Christ;"* It is never enough to be grateful that things are no worse than they are. Remember that all things do work together for good. - *Romans 8:28* - God didn't say all things are good, He said all things work together **for** good. **Realize that you belong to God, and it is always his reputation that is at stake in the events of your life.** – *(Psalms 23:3).* God is bigger than any problem that we may encounter and has the solution for every problem. - Isaiah 9:6 *"... and his name shall be called Wonderful, Counsellor, The mighty God, The everlasting Father, The Prince of Peace."*

② *Secondly* try to identify the **cause** of the problem. Did this problem occur because of something I did or didn't do? Does it reveal some character flaw in me? Does it reveal that I have the wrong attitude? (*Philippians 2:5*) Does it reflect a problem in my relationship with God? Did this problem occur because of the actions of someone else?

Did God send this problem into my life to help conform me into the image of Christ? - *Romans 8:29*

③ *Third,* try to determine the **lesson** that God is attempting to teach through this problem. What does God want me to learn from this lesson? - *Romans 8:29* - What does God want me to share with others from this lesson? - *2Corinthians 1:4* - How can this lesson make me, or those around me more Christ like? Jesus grew in every area of life. (physically, mentally, socially, and spiritually) - Luke 2:52 - *⁵²And Jesus increased in **wisdom** and **stature**, and in favour with **God** and **man**.* That is what God desired for His "only begotten son" - *John 1:14* - and what He desires for "his adopted sons". - *Romans 8:15.* Problems are often the defining occurrences in our life and as with so many other things, they can cause us to learn and grow, or they can destroy us. God will never allow a problem into our life that we cannot handle, through His grace. (1Corinthians 10:13 – *"There hath no temptation(trial) taken you but such as is common to man: but God is faithful, who will not suffer you to be tempted (tried) above that ye are able; but will with the temptation(trial) also make a way to escape, that ye may be able to bear it."* & Philippians 4:13 – *"I can do all things through Christ which strengtheneth me."*) We may have many problems that we do not like, and "all things may not be good" in our life. Rest assured, however, that "all things do **work** together **for** good". Learn to think of problems as friends, who are allowed into your life, to help you mature in Christ.

Chapter 8

Bitterness as it relates to our Home and Family

In Colossians 3:19 – *"Husbands, love your wives, and be not bitter against them."* the Apostle Paul admonishes husbands to refrain from **bitterness** toward their wives, and in Ephesians 6:4 – *"And, ye fathers, provoke not your children to wrath: but bring them up in the nurture and admonition of the Lord."* he says for fathers not to provoke their children to wrath. Both of these admonitions relate to **bitterness**, or resentment, or unresolved anger. Everything that I have said previously, in regard to **bitterness,** certainly applies to the home and family. In reality, most **bitterness** is pointed toward those closest to us. There is no special instruction for bitterness in a family, as opposed to **bitterness** between individuals. The answer is simply to take care of all **bitterness** in a Biblical fashion. Learn to apply the Scriptural truths we have discussed previously to deal with any bitterness currently in your life, and to prevent any future bitterness from occurring.

As with anything, prevention of a problem is always less painful and costly than the cure. I am convinced, that the **bitterness** allowed to develop in a home or family is the direct result of ignorance about, or rebellion toward, Biblical instructions regarding ourselves and our families. We are not born with the knowledge and wisdom to be husbands, wives, moms, or dads. This is a learned behavior, and the learning must come from the Word of God. With these things in mind let's look at God's program for a successful home and family.

Basic Needs in a Biblical marriage:

LEAVING

Lets begin with the basic laws of marriage from Scripture. The **first law** of God, in relation to marriage is the law of *Leaving* ...... this law applies to **both** husband and wife. In Genesis 2:24 – *"Therefore shall a man **leave** his father and his mother, and shall cleave unto his wife: and they shall be one flesh."* & Ephesians 5:31 – *"For this cause shall a man **leave** his father and mother, and shall be joined unto his wife, and they two shall be one flesh."* God is telling us that we are not ready for marriage until we are ready to *leave* the support, protection, and care of our parents in material matters. God commands that a man take care of his own household. (1 Timothy 5:8 - *[8]But if any provide not for his own, and specially for those of his own house, he hath denied the faith, and is worse than an infidel."*) If you are not ready to *leave* the provision and protection of your parents, then you are not ready to enter into the marriage relationship. I believe that it also means we are to *leave* all those things in the past that are potentially harmful to the marriage. We must, also, be willing to give up things in the present that are potentially damaging, or destructive to the marriage relationship. If there are habits, or routines that will adversely affect the well being of your life's partner these must go by the wayside. Successful marriage is a continuing system of compromises, on both sides of the aisle. Love is "the willingness to give, to meet the needs of another, without asking anything in return" - *(John 3:16)*. Is this the kind of unconditional love that dominates your relationship, or is what you call love, selfish and self-centered, which is not love at all.

CLEAVING

The **next law** of God is the law of ***Cleaving*** ..... this law also applies to **both** husband and wife – (Genesis 2:24 - *[24]Therefore shall a man leave his father and his mother, and shall **cleave** unto his wife: and they shall be one flesh.* & Ephesians 5:21, 31 – *"[21]Submitting yourselves one to another in the fear of God. [31]For this cause shall a man leave his father and mother, and shall be **joined** unto his wife, and they two shall be one flesh.")* These Scriptures teach us that there are several things that constitute the binding force, or glue in our marriage. First and foremost we must ***cleave*** to God. This is the binding force that will hold your marriage together when all else fails. The more tightly two people cling to God, the more tightly they will cling to one another. I realize that I am treading on thin ice with this next proposition, but I believe with all my heart that it is an imperative from God that we ***cleave*** to our marriage vows. These are sacred promises, made to each other, in the witness of God, and man. When we break our vows we break a sacred, and legal agreement, and thus we break the law, and heart of God. In a healthy marriage relationship, husband and wife will also cling to one another. When your friends desert you, and your children leave you, and your job bores you, and your strength fails you .... you will still have each other. Begin early in your marriage to build ties that will bind you together for a lifetime. After all, that is what you promised in the first place as you stood before man and God. Make plans that will successfully carry you through life together.

Careers are wonderful, children are great, grandchildren are marvelous, but you need each other more than any of these. Our children understood from a very early age that they always took third place in our lives. God was first, our relationship was second, and they were third. Career was somewhere after that.

God says that you are **_one flesh,_** and separation or divorce means a painful tearing of that flesh. This inevitably leaves wounds, and scars. Divorce should never be considered, when there is **ANY** other recourse.

LOVE
God's **third law** of marriage is my favorite. It is the law of **_Loving_** .... this command is directed primarily toward the **husband** – (Ephesians 5:25, 28 & 33 – "*[25]Husbands, **love** your wives, even as Christ also loved the church, and gave himself for it; [28]So ought men to **love** their wives as their own bodies. He that **loveth** his wife loveth himself. [33]Nevertheless let every one of you in particular so **love** his wife even as himself...")*
Christ illustrates this law in His unconditional *love* for His Church and us personally. The Apostle Paul tells us that husbands are to *love* their wives in exactly the same way that Christ *loves* the Church. There is certainly not room here to discuss in detail, how our Savior *loves* the Church, but there are two overriding principles that are very obvious. He *loved* the Church so much that He died for it historically. He also *loves* it so much that He lives for it daily. I truly believe that the latter is the more difficult for Him, and for us as husbands.

BITTER WATER AND BARREN LIVES

Dying is a onetime thing, and for the Christian, simply a change in location, not an end of our existence. Living for someone on a continual basis, day after day, can become a tremendous struggle. Just stop, and realize, for a moment what God, in the person of the Holy Spirit must tolerate daily in our lives. I imagine this makes putting up with our wife, or husband a simple matter. Not only are husbands to *love* their wives as Christ *loves* the Church, but they are to *love* them in the same manner as they *love* themselves. To help us understand this, God uses two very descriptive words. In Ephesians 5:29 – (*For no man ever yet hated his own flesh; but **nourisheth** and **cherisheth** it, even as the Lord the church:*) **_Nourish_** means to rear up to maturity through feeding, and teaching. [According to 1Corinthians 14:35 – *"And if they will learn anything, let them ask their husbands at home:..."*the wife's spiritual condition is largely the responsibility of the husband]. Husband you are the Spiritual leader in your home, and the Spiritual condition of your wife and children is something for which you must answer to God. God also uses the term **cherish**. **_Cherish_** means to soften by warmth. (This word was often used in Greek literature to describe a hen hatching her chicks.) I guarantee you that treating her with warmth, will soften your wife much more quickly, than if you are treating her coldly. If you want a warm, loving wife, you must be a warm, loving husband.

God next says that if you really *love* her, you need to treat her, as you want her to treat you. In 2Corinthians 9:6 – *"But this I say, He which soweth sparingly shall reap also sparingly; and he which soweth bountifully shall reap also bountifully. &* Luke 6:38 – *"Give, and it shall be given unto you; good measure, pressed down, and shaken together, and running over, shall men give into your bosom. For with the same*

measure that ye mete withal it shall be measured to you again.
The law of sowing and reaping can be a wonderful, or a terrible
law, depending on what you are sowing. Husband, are you
sowing *love*, kindness, gentleness, forgiveness, and patience, or
are you sowing anger, bitterness, jealousy, and grudging. You
will get back what you sow, **in greater measure**, and this is a
promise of God.

RESPECT

The **fourth law** that God gives us, regarding the marriage
relationship, is the law of ***Respect*** ..... this command is directed
toward the **wife**, but it is very essential that the husband *respect*
his wife, just as she is commanded to *respect* him. We find the
Apostle Paul dealing with the subject of *Respect* in his
letter to the Ephesians 5:22, 24 & 33 – *"²²Wives, **submit**
yourselves unto your own husbands, as unto the Lord.
²⁴Therefore as the church is **subject** unto Christ, so let the wives
be to their own husbands in every thing. ³³Nevertheless let every
one of you in particular so love his wife even as himself; and
the wife see that she reverence (**respect**) her husband."*

In this chapter he mentions three words that fall under the
category of *respect*. He talks about ***Submission*** which I believe
relates to a yielding of your rights to God, and then trusting
Him to return them in the form of privileges through your
husband . This is a willingness to follow a person out of love. I
believe this is first talking about her love for Christ, and
secondarily about her love for her husband. The next area of
respect is in the area of ***Subjection***. This can best be described
as a willingness to follow guidelines and instructions because of
love. Again, I am speaking about the wife's love for Christ first,
and then her love for the husband God has given her.

Position yourself under God's ordained leadership, and pray for God to lead your husband, so your husband can lead you biblically. In verse 33 God speaks of ***obedience*** out of *respect*. View your husband as the tool God is using to help build character and integrity into your life and his. Based on Ephesians 5:21 – *"Submitting yourselves one to another in the fear of God."* We are to submit to one another. The husband is to submit to the wife's need for love and protection, and the wife is to submit to the husband's need for respect and leadership. As I understand the curse placed on all mankind, in the book of Genesis, the wife who wants to lead is command to follow and the man who just wants to relax is commanded to lead.

We must realize that this is all to be done for the joy set before us in being obedient to the Lord. – (Hebrews 12:2 – *"Looking unto Jesus the author and finisher of our faith; who for the joy that was set before him endured the cross, despising the shame, and is set down at the right hand of the throne of God."*) Only a fool would believe that Christ enjoyed His death on the cross. He submitted to God for the joy of purchasing our eternal soul.

Basic ingredients in a Biblical marriage:

JESUS CHRIST

Another important deterrent to bitterness in the marriage relationship is an understanding of the **basic ingredients** God requires in a marriage. The **first** and most obvious ingredient in any marriage is *Jesus Christ*. In *Psalms 127:1* the Bible says, "that unless the Lord builds the home, our labors are simply in vain". Let me list some of the key factors required to have a Christ centered home;

⇒   Both husband and wife must know Christ as their **Lord**
and **Savior**.   *1Corinthians 11:3*
1.   Christ must be the *obvious* head of the home.
2.   The head of the *woman* is to be the man.
3.   The head of the *man* is to be Christ.

⇒   Christ must be the binding force in any marriage.
1.   The *husband* must know and love the Lord.
2.   The *wife* must know and love the Lord.

⇒   The *communal* love of Christ for us, and our love for
Him, and each other, is the only bond that can keep a
husband and wife together through all the trials of life
and marriage. Christ must be the *wisdom* and direction in
the marriage relationship.
1.   Through *prayer*.
2.   Through reading and heeding the *scripture*.
3.   Through *submission* to the Holy Spirit.

LOVE

The **second** ingredient in a Biblical marriage is real *love* for one another. In *Ephesians 5:25* God tells the husband to love his wife and in *Titus 2:4* he tells the wife to love her husband. To truly understand what Biblical love really is, we need to first discover what it isn't.

BITTER WATER AND BARREN LIVES

Love is not:

Real love is not ***Physical*** attraction ..... This is neither wrong nor sinful, and those who are really in love will be attracted to one another physically, but physical attraction alone is not love. Real love is not ***Lust*** ..... This is wrong, and sinful, and selfish, and should never be mistaken for Love. Love and lust are exact opposites. Love is kind, considerate, and selfless, while lust is selfish, inconsiderate, unkind, and contrary to the Word of God. Biblical love is not ***Personal Desire*** ..... Love must be based on God's *will* not my *want*. It has been my experience that much of what we want is outside of God's will, and often harmful to our life and ministry. God said that He would supply our needs, as we commit our lives to Him, and His will. He never said He would give us what we want! Love should never be confused with ***Sympathy*** ..... Feeling sorry for the conditions or circumstances of another is not wrong, but neither is it the basis on which to build a lifelong marriage relationship. Based on the word of God, I believe that people need help much more than they need sympathy, and a marriage based on sympathy is certainly not a marriage that can be of help to anyone.

What God says real love is:

Real love, on the other hand, is defined for us in *John 3:16* and further amplified in *1Corinthians 13:4-7*. Biblical love is the willingness to *give* to meet the needs of another without any thought of repayment. Love is an intense and difficult emotion to define and to deal with but God's word aptly defines this elusive entity. Let's take a brief tour through *1Corinthians 13*, and look at some of the things God says about real love.

Love is; *1 Corinthians 13:4-7*

⟹ ___Patient___ - Willing to wait on, and understand another. (*v.4*)

⟹ ___Kind___ - Always considerate of the feelings of another. (*v.4*)

⟹ ___Not Envious___ - Delighted about the talents, or blessings of another. (*v.4*)

⟹ ___Not Self-centered___ - Always centered on another. (*v.4*)

⟹ ___Not Rude___ - Reflected in politeness . (*v.5*)

⟹ ___Not Selfish___ - Meeting the needs of another first. (*v.5*)

⟹ ___Not Irritable___ - Not getting angry at every situation. (*v.5*)

⟹ ___Not Grudging___ - Making up quickly. (*v.5*)

⟹ ___Not Unjust___ - Always fair, and kind, and just. (*v.6*)

⟹ ___Loyal___ – Love can best be measured by its loyalty. (*v.7*)

COMMUNICATION

Marriage has a **third** vital ingredient, which is good ___communication___. To better understand communication, and especially good communication, lets look at some basic facts about communication. You cannot, ___not___ communicate. A look, a gesture, a shrug all says something about you, and something to the other person. Often silence speaks more loudly than words. There are many ___levels___ of communication. There is the ***content,*** which is what you actually say, but there is also the ***context,*** which is what you actually mean. Next is our ***attitude***, or the way in which we say, or imply something. Our ***attitude*** is often determined by how we *feel* mentally, emotionally, or physically, at the time we are trying to communicate. Often the actual meaning of what we say, gets distorted because of our **attitude**. A **denotative** meaning is exactly what we say, while a **connotative** meaning is the result of hinting, or suggesting something that may, or may not be true. We must also, always, take into consideration such things as **cultural** differences, which include our sex, race, religion, nationality, and the environment in which we were reared, and in which we now live. These can all affect our meaning, and our understanding.

There is much **discrepancy** in communication. Sometimes communication can be very contradictory via the same level, (*I feel great except for this headache*) or via different levels. (*Saying you are sad while smiling*) There is **ambiguous** communication, (*Not clear and concise in meaning*) **paradoxical** communication, (*I demand you be the boss*) and what I like to call **response dilemma**. (*Everything said is simply a reaction to provocation*) Another real dilemma in communication is when we use **implications** as opposed to simple statements, or questions.

> (*"Do you still abuse your wife?"* or
> *"Have you stopped getting drunk?"* or
> *"Do you still drive too fast?"*)

Why does communication break down? I believe that there are a myriad of reasons, but I would like to list just a few of the more prominent.

◊ We build **barriers** because of guilt, or anger.
◊ We are afraid, or **unwilling** to share our thoughts, and feelings with others.

◊ We are ***impatient,*** or unconcerned with others.
◊ We distrust the ***motives,*** or intentions of others.
◊ We are not ***sure*** of what to say, or how to say it.
◊ We are ***fearful*** of being misunderstood.
◊ We are afraid that no one can really ***understand,*** or help us.
◊ We are ***unwilling*** to chance a negative response.
◊ We are ***unsure*** about our own motives.
◊ We have a negative, and/or critical ***attitude*** toward others.

How can a husband and wife have good, clear communication?

⇒ Find special ***times*** to talk that are good, and comfortable for both of you.
⇒ Never lose your ***temper,*** but when you do, make up quickly.
   1. Never go to bed angry. *Ephesians 4:26*
   2. You take the initiative and apologize, no matter who is at fault. *Matthew 5:23-25*
⇒ Make sure your ***attitude,*** and ***motives*** are proper. *Matthew 7:1-5*
⇒Allow ***time,*** for your partner to react. *Don't push*
⇒ Always be ***truthful,*** but kind and loving. *Ephesians 4:15*
⇒ ***Pray*** about your communication.
   1. Pray for ***wisdom*** to communicate.
   2. Pray for an ***understanding*** spirit in communication.
   3. Pray for ***patience*** when communicating.

> **NOTE:** There are two magical phrases in communication *"I Am Sorry"* and *"I Love You"*.

MATURITY

The **fourth** ingredient in a healthy and Spiritual marriage relationship is *__maturity__*. Maturity is the ability to put off immediate gratification for the sake of God's glory and another's good. In 1Corinthians 13:11 – *"When I was a child, I spake as a child, I understood as a child, I thought as a child: but when I became a man, I put away childish things."* the Apostle Paul, tells us to grow up. Marriage is for adults, and there is no age that determines adulthood. Adulthood is an *attitude*, and that means we are to conform to the *attitude* of Christ (*Philippians 2:5*). Immaturity is a major problem in many marriages, and often the cause of resentment, and bitterness in the relationship. Some of the problems associated with *immaturity* are very obvious. Immaturity causes a person to be selfish and *self-centered*. It causes us to reject, or neglect our *responsibility*, and it robs us of a deep, and open *relationship* with one another. Since immaturity is such a problem lets look at some of the ways to develop maturity in our life, and relationships. First, I believe that we need to work hard at *overcoming* selfishness and self-centeredness in our life by concentrating on the needs of one another, and by developing the unselfish *attitude* of Christ (*Philippians 2:5*). Learn to *give* rather than *trade* in your marriage relationship. A marriage based on a 50/50 relationship will soon dissolve, in divorce, along those same lines of division. Marriage must be 100% on both sides, if it is to have a chance at success. Accept the place of responsibility you have chosen, and rejoice in it.

As a **husband** you are now the servant/leader in Spiritual and administrative matters. God has called you to be the *head* of your wife in the same manner as Christ is the head of the Church. (*Ephesians 5:23*) Husband ..... **GROW UP** ..... deal with your immaturity, and bitterness ..... you are to be the *strength* in social, and spiritual situations, and to act as your wife's protector, and provider in the areas of mental, emotional, and physical needs ..... God wants to use you, and your family to serve Him.

The **wife** also has some vital areas of maturity to deal with. As a wife you have added several vital new responsibilities to your life, and perhaps compounded your career. New things have come into your life. You are a wife, maybe a mother, and perhaps have a career outside the home. These thing are difficult enough when you are mature, they are impossible when you are immature. Wife .... **GROW UP** .... deal with your immaturity, and bitterness ..... you have vital needs to fill in your home and family .... God wants to use you, and your family to serve Him.

SUBMISSION

The **fifth** ingredient in a Biblical marriage relationship is **submission**. In 1Corinthians 11:3 – *"But I would have you know, that the head of every man is Christ; and the head of the woman is the man; and the head of Christ is God"*. the Apostle Paul gives us what has been commonly called, "God's chain of command" or "corporate structure". This covers several aspects, and areas of submission. It says that Christ is in submission to God, that the husband is to be in submission to Christ, and that the wife is to be in submission to the husband. In *Ephesians 5:21,* Paul says that the husband and wife are to be in submission to each other.

To better understand these three areas of submission lets look at each individually.

BIBLICAL SUBMISSION:

❶ Husband and wife are to be in *submission* to one another. Ephesians 5:21 – *"Submitting yourselves one to another in the fear of God."*) Husbands should submit to the wife's need for *love* and **protection**. *(Ephesians 5:25, 28, 31, and 33)*, and the wife should submit to the husband's need for **respect** and **leadership** *(Ephesians 5:22, 23, 24, and 33)*. Both husband and wife must realize that two unique individuals have been fused into one unit called a *family - Ephesians 5:33*. This does not mean that you can no longer have *individual* interests, and goals in life. It does mean, however, that you can no longer do those things that *adversely* affect the well being of your life's partner.

Again, let me say, that a successful marriage is a series of compromises and loving submission. Both husband and wife must learn to give, as well as get, in the marriage relationship.

❷ The husband is first, and foremost to be in *submission* to Christ. *Ephesians 5:1; & James 4:7.* He is to *observe* God's law, and to obey God's will, in every area of his life, as an example to his family. He is to *respect* God's church by his attendance, and involvement. He is to *minister* to God's people by loving them, and meeting their physical, emotional and Spiritual needs. He should also set the example of respect, and consideration for God's pastor. He is to be a generous steward with his *time*, his *talent*, his *testimony*, his *treasure* and his *thanksgiving* to God. If a husband is to lead his family, he must be sure he is following Christ. The husband is the *head* of the wife - *Ephesians 5:23* in the same manner as Christ is the *head* of the Church. This is a corporate structure under a spiritual directive.

It does **not** infer *superiority*, it does, however, dictate *leadership*. - 1Corinthians 16:13 – *"Watch ye, stand fast in the faith, quit (behave) you like men, be strong. ")*. The Bible also teaches us that the husband is to be the wife's *provider and protector* - *Ephesians 5:23*. Gentlemen, God has not called you to *leisure*, He has called you to *leadership*. I believe that this protection extends to all realms of life, which would include; The *Physical, Mental, Emotional, Material, Spiritual, and Sexual* areas of our relationship with our wives. This protection is to *mimic* the protection of Christ in our lives.

The husband is to be deeply in *love* with his wife - *Ephesians 5:25*. This means that he is to love her in *word* and in *deed.* Words of love are wonderful, but like salvation, without the *works* of love, these words eventually become meaningless. The husband is to_*dedicate* his life to his wife - *Ephesians 5:25* just as Christ dedicated His life to His Church.   Christ loved the Church, and husbands are to love their *wives*. Christ lived for the *Church,* and husbands are to live for their *wives*.   Christ died for the *Church,* and husbands are to *dedicate* their life to their *wife.* I fully understand that Christ must come first in all things but that is a "given" in this discussion. The husband is to *treat* his wife as he desires to be *treated* – Ephesians 5:28 – *"So ought men to love their wives as their own bodies. He that loveth his wife loveth himself."* Whatever we *sow* is what we *reap* – Galatians 6:7 – *"Be not deceived; God is not mocked: for whatsoever a man soweth, that shall he also reap."* Whatever we *give* is what we *get* – Luke 6:38 –*"Give, and it shall be given unto you; good measure, pressed down, and shaken together, and running over, shall men give into your bosom. For with the same measure that ye mete withal it shall be measured to you again."* If you want love, you must first give love. If you want kindness, you must first display kindness.

If you want forgiveness, you must first offer forgiveness. If, however, you want anger, jealousy, bitterness, and envy in your marriage, then just continue to display these traits, and they will come back, with interest.

❸ The wife is to be in *submission* to her husband. In *Genesis 3:16, Ephesians 5:22 & 1Peter 3:1* God wraps it in a simple package "Wives, submit yourselves unto your own husbands, as unto the Lord." God sets the precedent for submission by the wife. This is God's *command,* and if for no other reason, it should be followed as an act of obedience toward Him. This is not, however, the only reason. It is also God's *plan* for your happiness and well being *(Romans 8:28).* I recently read a wonderful book, by a lady named, P. B. Wilson entitled, "Liberated through Submission" in which she deals with the *joys* that a life of Biblical submission brings to both husbands and wives.

There does not seem to be an *exception* clause anywhere in scripture, because a life of submission is a life of fulfillment for both husband and wife. The wife's submission to her husband is the same relationship that **should** exist between the husband and Christ, and does exist between Christ and God. Always remember that Biblical submission is *obedience* to God, not *slavery* to your husband or wife.

The wife should be *submissive* in all areas of the relationship *Ephesians 5:22-24.* Obviously this does not apply to areas of *sin, immorality,* or *physical and emotional abuse.* In areas of *conflict* you must be careful to determine which command of God takes precedence *"Never make decisions based on supposition".* The wife needs to understand that her husband is to be recognized as the *strength* in the home - 1Peter 3:7 – *"Likewise, ye husbands, dwell with them according to knowledge, giving honour unto the wife, as unto the weaker vessel, and as being heirs together of the grace of life; that your prayers be not hindered."*

As a Biblical wife you should never try to *assume* the role of leader, nor ever try to *force* your husband into this position. If he refuses to accept the position of leadership that God has called him to, then you need to step back, and allow God to deal with him. Just simply look at the logic of the situation. If God cannot cause him to take his proper position, how can you imagine that you are capable of getting him to respond? You would have to be greater than God. The thing that normally happens is that you fail in the attempt, and become bitter over the situation. That only makes matters worse.

As a Godly wife you need to maintain your *purity* and *chastity* for your husband - *Ephesians 5:26-27.* Be careful not to *reveal* your body to anyone, but your own husband. Beware of seductive *clothing,* and seductive *behavior.* Do not *reveal* your marriage, and personal problems to anyone, but your husband. Obviously a trustworthy pastor, counselor, or physician, is an exception. You should, however, tell your husband first. Do not reveal intimate *secrets, fears,* and *dreams* that the two of you share, with anyone, except by mutual consent. The Apostle Paul says that the wife is to respect her husband in the same manner that the believer is to respect the *Lord - Ephesians 5:33.* This means that she is to be *faithful, loving, kind, respectful* and *submissive.*

Bitterness in the marriage relationship is dealt with in the same way, as any other relationship. The only difference is the unique and special relationship that exists between a husband and wife. God says, "that you are one flesh" which means that anything you do, directly, and intimately, affects your spouse.

My suggestion for dealing with **bitterness** problems between a husband and wife is, first to get by your self, and list all of the areas of bitterness that you have toward your spouse. After you have made the list, read it over carefully, ask God to forgive you for each of these areas of **bitterness**, and then destroy the list.

Next, sit down with your spouse (find a convenient time, and quite place), and begin by having prayer together. Holding hands, and facing one another, you should each ask the other to forgive you for your **bitterness** (without disclosing any specific hurts, or offenses) toward them, and to forgive you for failing as a *"help meet"* in the marriage. This should really be done between husband and wife before you attempt to seek forgiveness from anyone else. After you have dealt with all of the **bitterness** in your life, you will gain an emotional freedom from others, and a new and wonderful attachment to your spouse that never existed before.

Chapter 9

Bitterness as it relates to our Children

The Bible also has much to say about **bitterness,** as it relates to our children. I have found parents are capable of being **bitter** toward their children, and that children can be **bitter** toward their parents. As in the marriage relationship, this bitterness stems from a lack of knowledge about the Biblical development of our children. In *Luke 2:52* the Bible says "Jesus increased in wisdom and stature, and in favor with God and man." This tells us that He developed mentally, physically, Spiritually, and socially. Our children are to develop the same way if their life is to be well balanced. That development is the responsibility of the parents, as they allow God to instill wisdom in them, through the influence and work of His Holy Spirit.

Sometimes the birth of children is well planned, and orchestrated, but more often than not they are a bit of a surprise. Remember that no matter which condition exists, they are a gift from God ..... God's special gift to us carries with it some special responsibilities, as well as some wonderful joys. According to the word of God, children should be a real *strength* to our family - *Psalms 127:3-5.* They are Gods *gift.* *.....A heritage not a handicap, invaluable not inconvenient.... a reward not a regret ..... fruit not frustration ..... arrows not accidents.* They are Gods *will* for your life.

BITTER WATER AND BARREN LIVES

God says in Genesis 1:28 – *"And God blessed them, and God said unto them, Be fruitful, and multiply,......"* and He always knows best. From conception you begin to store memories and experiences that will last a lifetime. The real joy in this gift comes through the years of growing, and maturing together. From conception, the responsibility for these lives belongs to *both* parents. –

Proverbs 1:8 & 31:1 – *"⁸My son, hear the instruction of thy father, and forsake not the law of thy mother:" "¹The words of king Lemuel, the prophecy that his mother taught him.".*

The responsibility of care and protection is found in;
2Corinthians 12:14 – *".......for the children ought not to lay up for the parents, but the parents for the children."* &
1Samuel 2:19 - *"Moreover his mother made him a little coat, and brought it to him from year to year, when she came up with her husband to offer the yearly sacrifice."*

The responsibility for training and discipline is found in;
Proverbs 22:6 – *"Train up a child in the way he should go: and when he is old, he will not depart from it."* &
2Timothy 1:5 – *"When I call to remembrance the unfeigned faith that is in thee, which dwelt first in thy grandmother Lois, and thy mother Eunice; and I am persuaded that in thee also."*

There are many common problems most *parents* face. We continually deal with a failure to *communicate* properly, because we lack time, or just refuse to take time, for communication with our children. We are sometimes guilty of talking down to children, and often we fail to deal with each child as an individual. We display a lack of *confidence, trust* and *respect* for the child, and this shows up in the ways that we find fault with what they do, and the ways we put them down for their efforts, and endeavors. We often compare them with other children, and sometimes even other children in their own family (brothers & sisters). We fail to show definite *leadership* in the child's life, by failing to promote their individual identity.

We push them instead of gently pointing the way, and by not presenting life's alternatives fairly. As parents we should know what we desire for our children in the way of a future, but we must allow them to choose that future, based upon good, and Godly biblical guidelines. It is our responsibility to lay down those guidelines in a fair and impartial manner so that God is able to move with certainty in their lives.

We also fail to recognize, and biblically deal with the seemingly small *problems* our children face every day. Their problems may not seem important to us, and they certainly can be an extreme irritant, as we deal with the bigger issue of life but, remember their problems are just as important to them as ours are to us. We need to make their problems a priority, before they do, truly, get out of hand. All children deal with the problem of *rebellion*, to one degree or another – 1Samuel 15:23 – *"For rebellion is as the sin of witchcraft, and stubbornness is as iniquity and idolatry"*.

We first need to understand the causes of rebellion in a child, or even in an adult. They are seeking attention, and are dealing with self-pity and selfishness, or they are just simply rejecting authority in their life because their authority figures have disappointed them. Children also, often, deal with feelings of *inadequacy* in their life. This may be because parents, or others, constantly tell them they are inadequate, and thus create in them a real inferiority complex.   These feelings of *inadequacy* may be rooted in laziness, or a lack of motivation on their part. This can stem from a lack of *__identity__*. They want to know who they are, where they are going, why they are here, and what God's will and plan for their life is all about. For these problems, and many others, which constitute the roots of bitterness, there are some workable, biblical *__solutions.__*

COMMUNICATION

First of all, learn to communicate with your children. Listen to them, talk with them .... not at them, and learn to respect their opinions. They may be a lot smarter than you think. *After all they are your children.* Help your children to develop *confidence* in God, and themselves – Philippians 4:13 - *"I can do all things through Christ which strengtheneth me."* Don't compare them to others. Find things they can excel in. Give credit where credit is due. Offer CONSTRUCTIVE criticism only. Help them to understand and accomplish Gods *will* in their life - Deuteronomy 6:5-7 – *"And thou shalt love the LORD thy God with all thine heart, and with all thy soul, and with all thy might. ⁶And these words, which I command thee this day, shall be in thine heart: ⁷And thou shalt teach them diligently unto thy children, and shalt talk of them when thou sittest in thine house, and when thou walkest by the way, and when thou liest down, and when thou risest up."*

IDENTIFICATION

Promote their individual identities. Help them to set definite goals in life, and always present life's alternatives fairly so they can make well-informed decision about their life, and future. We must point without pushing. We must inform without oppressing. We must love without smothering.

DISCIPLINE

Use proper modes and methods of *discipline*. Establish clearly the reason for discipline. Let God work on their heart first, and then rationally discuss the issue of discipline (send to room, etc.). When administering discipline you should naturally display parental grief, and thus associate love with discipline. In all forms of discipline, always make God's word the final authority. There have been many debates on corporal punishment so I will simply relate to you what God's word says;

Proverbs 10:13, 13:24, 22:15, 23:13,14, & 29:15;

[13]In the lips of him that hath understanding wisdom is found: but a rod is for the back of him that is void of understanding.
[24]He that spareth his rod hateth his son: but he that loveth him chasteneth him betimes.
[15]Foolishness is bound in the heart of a child; but the rod of correction shall drive it far from him.
[13]Withhold not correction from the child: for if thou beatest him with the rod, he shall not die. [14]Thou shalt beat him with the rod, and shalt deliver his soul from hell.
[15]The rod and reproof give wisdom: but a child left to himself bringeth his mother to shame.

Always use a neutral object for corporal punishment (Corporal punishment is now illegal in several states and as Christians we must obey the laws of the land). The hands you use for displaying affection and love should not be the instruments of discipline. Be very cautious, there is a very thin line between corporal punishment, and child abuse. We never have the right to abuse our children, or anyone else for that matter.

Comfort them after correcting them. Discuss the need for restitution if applicable. Evaluate your correction, and their response to make sure that the *"punishment fits the crime"*. Determine whether or not your correction resulted in a change of their attitude and actions. Remember, their behavior may be *bad*, but they are not *bad*. We teach more by our *walk* than our *talk*. The great pastor and preacher, D. L. Moody said, "Your children cannot hear the **whisper** of your words, for the **roar** of your life".

The Minnesota Crime Commission did a study on child development a few years ago, and came up with some startling results. Understand this is a secular study done by policemen, and educators, but it clearly shows the validity of the word of God in the rearing of our children.

Minnesota Crime Commissions says;

"Every baby starts life as a little savage. He is completely selfish and self-centered. He wants, what he wants, when he wants it, his bottle, his mother's attention, his playmates toys, his uncle's watch. Deny him these wants and he seethes with rage and aggressiveness, which would be murderous, were he not so helpless. He is dirty; he has no morals, no knowledge, and no developed skill. This means that all children are born delinquent and if allowed to continue in their self-centered world of infancy, given free reign to their impulsive action to satisfy each want, every child will grow up to be a criminal, a thief, a killer and a rapist."

On the other hand God says;

Proverbs 13:24 *"He that spareth his rod hateth his son: but he that loveth him chasteneth him betimes."*

Proverbs 22:15 *"Foolishness is bound in the heart of a child; but the rod of correction shall drive it far from him."*

Proverbs 29:15 *"The rod and reproof give wisdom: but a child left to himself bringeth his mother to shame."*

****

Elisa Morgan, president of MOPS International (Mothers of Pre-Schoolers), shared this insight into a child's view of the world:

Toddler's Creed

If I want it, it's mine.

If I give it to you and

change my mind later, it's mine.

If I can take it away from you, it's mine.

If I had it a little while ago, it's mine.

If it's mine, it will never belong to anyone else, no matter what.

If we are building something together, all the pieces are mine.

If it looks like mine, it is mine.

BITTER WATER AND BARREN LIVES

I would like to summarize this entire book with a few simple thoughts, which perhaps you can memorize and personalize into your own life. Remember, **"your problem is not your problem, your problem is how you respond to your problem."** Everything is wrapped up in our *attitude*. The Bible says, (Philippians 2:5) *We are to have the same attitude as Christ.* Our *attitude* determines our *actions*, and if we have a **bitter** attitude, then we will be ruled by **bitter** actions. Learn to forgive, and forgive quickly. Learn to seek forgiveness, and seek it early. Deal with bitterness in the Biblical way, in each area of your life. Quit being **conformed** to the world, and start letting Christ **transform** you by the renewing of your mind - Romans 12:2 – *"And be not conformed to this world: but be ye transformed by the renewing of your mind, that ye may prove what is that good, and acceptable, and perfect, will of God."* This can only occur as you begin to worship, pray, read and study the Bible, and lead your family to do the same thing.

If you have just finished reading this book, you are probably a *"born-again"* (*John 3:1-8*) Christian. There is, however, the possibility that you have no idea what that phrase means or you have heard some negative comments about being *"born again"*. Let me take a moment to simplify what God is referring to when He tells Nicodemus that he must be *"born again"*. He says that the *"new birth"* occurs when an individual places their faith and trust in Jesus Christ as their Lord and Savior. This means nothing more and nothing less. If you have never received Jesus Christ as your Lord and Savior, I would like to share with you, God's plan for your eternal life. God says in Romans 3:23 *"For all have sinned, and come short of the glory of God;"* This means that we are all sinners, and need the salvation of Christ.

In Romans 6:23 He says *"For the wages of sin is death; but the gift of God is eternal life through Jesus Christ our Lord.)"*. Here he is saying that the final reward for a life dedicated to SIN is death, but the free gift of God is eternal life through Jesus Christ our Lord. In Romans 10:13 He says *"For whosoever shall call upon the name of the Lord shall be saved."* Here he is telling us that whoever asks the Lord for eternal life will be given that life eternally and immediately.

Salvation settles your sin debt to God for all eternity, but it doesn't solve every problem in this life. Both Peter in 1Peter 2:1, 2 – *"Wherefore laying aside all malice, and all guile, and hypocrisies, and envies, and all evil speakings, ²As newborn babes, desire the sincere milk of the word, that ye may grow thereby:"* and Paul in his letter to the Ephesians 4:31 - *"Let all **bitterness**, and wrath, and anger, and clamour, and evil speaking, be put away from you, with all malice: ³²And be ye kind one to another, tenderhearted, forgiving one another, even as God for Christ's sake hath forgiven you."* tells us to get rid of the **bitterness** in our lives. They are both talking to new Christians, which assures us that the **bitterness**, and **"emotional response patterns"** that we developed over a lifetime, followed us into salvation. So while salvation will solve your eternal problems and assure you of Heaven for all eternity, do not expect salvation to eliminate the **bitterness** in you soul ..... you must do that!

Salvation gives us the tools that we need to deal with our **bitterness**, but it does not automatically remove this soul poison that is hindering our ability to produce *fruit*.

BITTER WATER AND BARREN LIVES

With the advent of the *"new birth"* we have the Holy Spirit to guide us through God's instruction book (Bible) and we have the Church, Christian teachers, and friends to help and support us emotionally as we deal with these vital issues, and continue our quest for spiritual *fruit* in our lives and ministry.

Receive Christ as your Savior, follow Christ in Baptism, join a Bible preaching Church, deal with the *bitterness* in your life and get involved in a ministry of praying for and helping others.